Introduction

Academic Reading
and Writing Skills
for University Students

Kendall Hunt
publishing company

Deborah Blenkhorn
Kwantlen Polytechnic University

MW01139886

Cover image courtesy of Deborah Blenkhorn

publishing company

www.kendallhunt.com
Send all inquiries to:
4050 Westmark Drive
Dubuque, IA 52004-1840

Copyright © 2019 by Kendall Hunt Publishing Company

ISBN 978-1-5249-9190-6

All rights reserved. No part of this publication may be reproduced,
stored in a retrieval system, or transmitted, in any form or by any means,
electronic, mechanical, photocopying, recording, or otherwise,
without the prior written permission of the copyright owner.

Published in the United States of America

CONTENTS

SECTION 1

STUDY SKILLS FOR UNIVERSITY—A New Playing Field   1

SECTION 2

GRAMMAR—Working with the Building Blocks of Communication   27

SECTION 3

COMPOSITION STRATEGIES—The Art of Rhetoric   95

SECTION 4
RHETORICAL ANALYSIS—Reflections on Writing   125

SECTION 5:
WRITING RESEARCH ESSAYS—Charting Your Journey   147

ACKNOWLEDGEMENTS

I would like to thank my editing partner, H. L. Reynolds, and my life partner, Steve Forster, for their help and their faith in me.

Thanks also to Stefani DeMoss and Alec Keiper at Kendall Hunt for their encouragement and support.

Finally, I would like to express my gratitude to Robert Dearle for getting me involved in teaching Writing 1100 at Kwantlen Polytechnic University.

PREFACE

This book is intended to help students adjust to university-level English course requirements, and to prepare them for further postsecondary studies.

Beyond theoretical knowledge and explanations of concepts, the text features a number of practical exercises to provide hands-on experience and give opportunities for peer editing and instructor feedback.

You will see sections on Study Skills, Grammar, Composition, Rhetorical Analysis, Research, and Editing. Readings are provided in a separate section, as is an Appendix of Marking Terms.

I hope you find these materials helpful!

Deborah Blenkhorn
Kwantlen Polytechnic University
Surrey, British Columbia

INTRODUCTION

Writing in the Twenty-First Century, and Why It Still Matters

In today's world of online chat, video, auto-response boxes, and voice recognition software, why should we cling to the timeworn art of writing, especially when we can opt for modes of communication that seem to be less stressful?

In an academic environment, the evident answer is that most postsecondary courses require us to communicate, in written form, what we understand to others who are teaching and learning the materials at hand. Presentations and visuals will take us only part of the way to academic success—and even those materials, whether they be PowerPoint or Prezi, require some mastery of the written word to be most effective.

Essay writing remains an essential skill for university life across the disciplines, and those who enter postsecondary studies with a good grasp of how to write an academic paper are at a distinct advantage. Arguably, high school completion should guarantee that this skill is in place for students embarking on their first-year/freshman journey, but the reality is somewhat different, as (not to mention individual student learning curves) schools and teachers vary in their priorities and their approach.

As an instructor, I'll never forget asking a first-year student, who seemed baffled by the instruction to "write an essay" on a topic related to a reading assignment, what I thought was the rhetorical question of whether grade 12 English had covered any reading or essay writing.

"Well," was the response, "I think we were supposed to write an essay, but they changed it to a poster."

"And the reading?" I enquired.

"Well, we were going to be reading a book but they changed it to a movie."

"What was the movie?" I asked, almost afraid to hear the answer.

"*Free Willy!*"

Now, when I recall my *"Free Willy"* moment as a teacher, every time a new semester begins, I think about all the different experiences learning about strategies for reading and writing that my students bring to first-year university English.

Starting with the basics of grammar, sentence structure, and paragraphing, we often need to check in with our sense of what works—and what we need to work on—in our writing. And not everyone is equally comfortable or adept in the university classroom: when we are on the receiving end of academic materials, we can benefit from honing our listening and note-taking skills.

By learning to produce clear, straightforward prose, we can avoid some of the ambiguities that can muddle our attempts at communication. Understanding the basics of argument will help us move further toward a critical evaluation of what we read; the writings we will examine epitomize creative use of the principles and strategies of rhetoric we will explore and analyze.

As we read through these masterworks, and pursue further research with a view to incorporating secondary sources into our own compositions, these and other writings by expert practitioners can give us valuable insights, and serve as touchstones for our own progress through the process of becoming a better communicator.

The intent of this book is to create a resource that allows you, during what can be a challenging transition into the university reading and writing environment, to benefit from decades of experience of teaching and learning. By the time you finish this course, you should be confident that you can read with comprehension, present your ideas with assurance, write clear and concise prose—and, ultimately, be your own best editor.

Enjoy the challenge—and the rewards—of the reading and writing process throughout your academic experience, and beyond.

Deborah Blenkhorn, B.A. (Hons.) / B.Ed., M.A.

STUDY SKILLS FOR UNIVERSITY—
A New Playing Field

As we move away from traditional, standard learning paradigms, today's students come onto the playing field of learning from a wide variety of learning styles. The sports metaphor of a playing field often includes the idea of fairness and equality: is it a level playing field? The simple answer is that it is not—but we can ensure that everyone has the right equipment and training, and the best possible chance to succeed.

In the twenty-first century and in our increasingly international learning community, students may face particular challenges beyond those of previous generations. We may spend less time reading books and more time on screen, but has this phenomenon significantly changed our learning profiles in contemporary society?

As you read the following descriptions, ask yourself if any of the following learner profiles resonate with you, and prepare to write approximately three hundred words (a few short paragraphs) in response on the blank pages following. We'll get a sense of individual and class skills from this diagnostic exercise.

Some students seem to learn best when they can read the information they need to absorb in preparation for their academic tasks; these _textual learners_ are the ones who request lecture notes and supplementary readings.

In what way(s) would you consider yourself to be a textual learner?

_____

_____

In contrast, _auditory learners_ prefer an in-person explanation and may find that hearing what they need to know is the most efficient strategy for them.

In what way(s) would you consider yourself to be an auditory learner?

_____

_____

Others, _experiential learners_, thrive in a learning environment that is highly interactive and discovery-based; these students are particularly drawn to participate in class discussions and group work projects.

In what way(s) would you consider yourself to be an experiential learner?

_____

_____

Still others are _visual learners_ who like to see information represented graphically, with charts, diagrams, and pictures.

In what way(s) would you consider yourself to be a visual learner?

_____

_____

Of course, these categories are not mutually exclusive—you may be one or more of the types I've mentioned earlier—or you may feel that none of these labels fits precisely.

Any alternative ideas about describing your learning style?

_____

_____

_____

Knowing (or finding out) your learning style can help you target your best working strategies as a student; as we look at different listening and note-taking strategies in this section, we will consider which strategies work best for the different types of learners. The best way to discover which techniques are most effective is by attempting them in different contexts—perhaps in other classes besides English as well. During your time as a university student, you may well end up creating a hybrid system that is a combination of (my takes on) these traditional methods.

Feel free to experiment! Meanwhile, talk about the question on the next page with a partner or partners in class, then write about it.

Discussion and Writing Opportunity: What Type of Learner Are You? (Diagnostic Writing)

_____

_____

_____

_____

_____

_____

_____

_____

_____

_____

_____

_____

_____

_____

_____

_____

_____

_____

_____

_____

_____

_____

_____

_____

_____

_____

_____

_____

_____

_____

_____

_____

Listening and Note-Taking

Listening skills are crucial to success in university—if we don't understand what is being said, our notes will reflect this lack of clarity, and will have limited usefulness (or may even steer us wrong).

We can enhance our listening (and that of those around us) by quietly paying attention to what is happening in the class; the expectation in university classes is that you will listen quietly and refrain from any distracting use of technological devices.

Ideally, you will find it easy to understand your instructor during the classes, as well as your fellow students who are asking questions and presenting their own ideas at times. To check in with your comprehension skills, a dictation exercise can give you a sense of how challenging the listening process may be in class.

Dictation is a process whereby you simply write down exactly what you hear. Try to include what you feel is suitable punctuation; try to spell all words correctly; and, most importantly, try to understand the ideas in the piece that is being dictated. Afterward, by looking at the original passage, you can determine how accurately you were able to execute this exercise.

Understanding lecture materials will be crucial, so pay particular attention to the results of dictation from the instructor; it is also useful to do this exercise with a partner in class, as part of your learning will come from the interaction with your peers.

When you are dictating material to a partner, speak slowly and clearly; enunciate each word carefully (you may wish to look up some of the vocabulary in your chosen passage prior to reading it aloud; both traditional and online dictionaries give pronunciation cues).

Repeat each sentence (or part thereof in a longer sentence), and repeat the entire passage after you have finished. You and your partner can check each other's work by referring to the original passage selected.

The purpose of this exercise is not to achieve a perfect copy of a piece of writing, but to give you a sense of how accurately you are understanding and transcribing what you hear.

Speed is not the goal, but remember that real-time note-taking requires efficiency.

Here are some basic guidelines for listening and note-taking; feel free to add your own ideas at the bottom of the chart:

DO	DON'T
→ Turn off your phone during class; you are not available to take calls during this time (if you are truly in a potential emergency situation, such as a family member's medical emergency, reconsider whether you should be in class: true emergencies do not include work situations, picking someone up at the airport, etc.)	✗ Have your phone on silent/vibrate (it will still be a distraction); it is very hard to ignore if you know a message or call (or even an e-mail) has come in, and your looking at your phone during class is bound to be annoying to the instructor, whether a lecture, group work, or in-class exercise is in progress; similarly, do not listen to music when you need to listen
→ If you have questions or comments, put up your hand and ask the teacher, or jot down the points to raise later	✗ Talk to someone sitting near you (it will distract your fellow students and the instructor)
→ Have notepaper and a pen with you, or take notes on your laptop, opened to a file you have created, if permitted	✗ Look at anything, especially on screen, other than the notes you are making (unless directed otherwise by your instructor)
→ Make strategic use of a note-taking technique that works for you (see the suggestions in this chapter)	✗ Jot down only random notes or doodling; these will be unlikely to make sense as study tools when you look back at them later
→ Look at the instructor (or other presenter addressing the class); you may nod slightly to show your understanding as you make eye contact	✗ Be distracted by other people or activities (e.g., something happening in the hallway—you can shut the door to the classroom if it is noisy outside)
→ Continue to pay attention until the end of the session	✗ Start packing up early (no need to do this, as classes typically end ten minutes before the next class begins)

DICTATION 1 (from instructor) from Section 7

DICTATION 2 (from a peer) from Section 7

Charting

As you glance through most textbooks (including this one), you will see that the standard format of paragraphing is interrupted by graphic materials. Regardless of the subject matter, some of the information tends to be represented, as it is in this section and others, in chart form. What is the rationale behind this strategy?

As we skim through or look over pages of material, our eye is instinctively drawn to the charts as representing important points in an easy-to-grasp format. Many academics—as well as professionals in other fields—make use of charts (written on a board, projected on a screen, or included in handout materials) to supplement their lectures or presentations.

A manageable number of ideas are clearly sorted into categories in such a way as to promote our understanding of the concepts involved. Could we achieve the same clarity by using this strategy to create our own notes for recording material from university classes? Absolutely!

Unless you are simply copying a chart or setting one up according to given specifications (I sometimes provide a blank chart with a few basic headings to facilitate studying in preparation for exams in my courses), you will need to decide what makes sense to include and how to sort out the ideas you want to include.

For instance, the first sample chart provided here includes, along with boxes for headings at the top, five rows and three columns, which could be used to record the titles and authors of articles in one column, the main ideas in the second, and quotable quotes in the third—you may choose to make a chart that has a different structure for your own use.

The second sample chart is set up to show the "pro" (for) and "con" (against) sides of a debate, which may be particularly useful in circumstances where you are exploring various aspects of an argument or controversial issue, or if you are considering a counterpoint to the argument of an iconoclastic writer such as Thoreau.

Here's a quick overview of how the charting method dovetails with the learning profiles we identified earlier, with the bulleted item showing what may be the best fit:

Type of Learner	Advantage
Textual	Each block or column in the chart becomes a minitext
Auditory	As you hear ideas, you sort them into chartable components
Experiential	Charting works well as a group exercise to follow up a lesson
• Visual	You create a graphic representation of organized thoughts

PRACTICE EXERCISE

Use the first chart template to record the titles and authors of articles from Section 7 in one column, the main ideas in the second, and quotable quotes in the third.

Use the second chart template to explore the PROs and CONs of an idea from one of the Readings, for example, Thoreau's "Walden" could lead you to consider the advantages and disadvantages of living in rural isolation.

CHART TEMPLATE 1

Name	Date
Subject	Page

Category 1	Category 2	Category 3
A.		
B.		
C.		
D.		
E.		

CHART TEMPLATE 2

Name	Date
Subject	Page

PROS	CONS

Sentence Method

Most people understand ideas best when they are expressed as complete thoughts.

The experience of looking back at your own notes and not having the same understanding of the ideas that you had at the time can be frustrating; you may also want to share your notes with others who struggle to get the meaning from your notes.

How we record our ideas can often be as important as what we record in the notes we take.

If you fear that your notes may not make sense when you look back at them later, the sentence method could be the most effective strategy for you.

A traditional method of recording complete thoughts, the sentence method encourages you to record ideas in a manner that represents syntactic integrity; whether the notes are in complete sentences or in point form, each (numbered, and double spaced if you wish) line has sufficient information to be easily read and understood—by the note-taker and by others—even after a lapse of days, weeks, or even months.

Sometimes, what you hear or read will already be in a sentence (or part thereof) that you have time to write down accurately during the note-taking phrase; if so, make sure you put the material in quotes. Make sure you identify the speaker or source, recording all relevant details.

This method requires significant effort at the note-taking stage, but may end up saving your time at the reviewing stage, especially when you are processing particularly dense, complex, or archaic material such as the writings of Aristotle or Locke.

Here's a quick overview of how the sentence method dovetails with the learning profiles we identified earlier, with the bulleted item showing what may be the best fit:

Type of Learner	Advantage
• Textual	You create your own textual material in a coherent form to read
Auditory	You can record the exact words a lecturer is saying, in quotes
Experiential	You can offer others an easy-to-understand account of the ideas
Visual	You can see each line on the page as a distinct point

PRACTICE EXERCISE

In the first Sentence Form Template, record some of Aristotle's thoughts on "Education" (from Section 7).

In the second Sentence Form Template, record some of Locke's views concerning "Human Understanding" (from Section 7).

"[T]he English language . . . becomes ugly and inaccurate
because our thoughts are foolish, but the slovenliness
of our language makes it easier for us to have foolish
thoughts. The point is that the process is reversible.
Modern English, especially written English, is full of
bad habits which spread by imitation and which can be
avoided if one is willing to take the necessary trouble. If
one gets rid of these habits one can think more clearly . . . "

—*George Orwell, "Politics and the English Language"*

SENTENCE FORM TEMPLATE 1

Name	Date
Subject	Page

1.
2.
3.
4.
5.
6.
7.
8.
9.
10.

SENTENCE FORM TEMPLATE 2

Name	Date
Subject	Page

1.

2.

3.

4.

5.

6.

7.

8.

9.

10.

Cornell Notes

Cornell Notes, which postsecondary students have been using since the 1940s, are the brainchild of Walter Pauk, who taught in the Faculty of Education at Cornell University.

Taking notes in this way while someone is lecturing can assure that you understand and retain the materials presented—a popular method of keeping handwritten lecture notes.

The system is based on the notion of identifying, isolating, and articulating key ideas and their supporting details. To use this system effectively, you need to instinctively grasp the difference between a main concept (say, vegetables) and illustrative examples (carrots, peas, and lettuce); bear in mind that the lecturer may furnish the illustrative materials and leave it to you to extrapolate (and subsequently recall) the generalities. You can try making these distinctions in some of Section 7, such as those by Emerson and Mill.

Of course, your professor may or may not be putting notes on a board or screen; those notes may include only key points or details, or a combination of both. Even if the professor provides handout materials or lecture notes, you will greatly increase your comprehension by using Cornell notes to record the information.

Here is a common method for using Cornell Notes: during class, write in the Notes section on the right side of the page; later, you can create or add to the Recall section of key points on the left; when studying or reviewing, do an overview in the Summary section.

By identifying each sheet of Cornell Notes clearly with your name, the subject, the date, and a page number, you ensure quick and accurate filing of your notes for future reference. Most importantly, you will be able to easily see which points are essential to the subject when it comes to studying for a test and/or writing an essay on the subject.

Here's a quick overview of how Cornell Notes dovetail with the learning profiles we identified earlier, with the bulleted item showing what may be the best fit:

Type of Learner	Advantage
Textual	You are producing your own readable resource
• Auditory	You can listen to the lecture attentively and modify notes later
Experiential	You can share and compare your notes with those of others
Visual	You are creating in chart form a record of important ideas

PRACTICE EXERCISE

On your first Cornell Notes Template, record main and subordinate points from Emerson's essay on "Language" (see Section 7). After comparing your work with that of a classmate, complete the summary section of the template.

On your second Cornell Notes Template, record main and subordinate points from Mill's essay on "Liberty" (see Section 7). After comparing your work with that of a classmate, complete the summary section of the template.

"[T]he secret of good writing is to strip every sentence to its cleanest components. Every word that serves no function, every long word that could be a short word, every adverb which carries the same meaning that is already in the verb, every passive construction that leaves the reader unsure of who is doing what—these are the thousand and one adulterants that weaken the strength of a sentence. And they usually occur, ironically, in proportion to education and rank."

—William Zinsser, "Simplicity"

CORNELL NOTES TEMPLATE 1

Name	Date
Subject	Page
Recall Column	Notes Column
(Key Points)	(Details)

SUMMARY

CORNELL NOTES TEMPLATE 2

Name	Date
Subject	Page
Recall Column	Notes Column
(Key Points)	(Details)

SUMMARY

Other Useful Techniques

Beyond these tried-and-true methods of note-taking, especially for those who find that writing something down—in any form—is a distraction from the material being presented, we can consider some alternative strategies.

For instance, students who have a documented learning challenge (which is on file with the institution and supported by an official letter to that effect) can have a note-taker (such as another student designated within the class) to record the content of the lectures.

In some cases, professors will provide lecture notes to supplement student learning. These notes can then be read over and understood when the student is better able to focus on them without the pressure of time. Of course, these are still notes, as such, in written (or typed) form. Can we think outside that box?

Technology gives us a few options—but you must ensure that you have permission (unless you are simply taking pictures of published materials for your own use).

Depending on the comfort level and preference of the lecturer, you may be able to record a lecture or parts thereof on your portable device. Most teachers have occasionally been recorded on audio and video, either with the support of a staff technician or by individual students on their own devices.

Some professors provide videotaped lectures on their course websites. And your fellow students may welcome the opportunity to have their presentations recorded so that they can watch them and self-evaluate. All of this is a matter of preference and comfort level on the part of whoever is presenting the material you want to record; never do so without asking, and always be prepared to take notes in another way.

At the very least, most people will not mind if you want to use the camera on your phone to take a picture of the screen or board at the front of the class, as long as you do so in a way that is not disruptive.

Here is our learning profile chart as it pertains to such alternatives:

Type of Learner	Advantage
Textual	You can transcribe important ideas subsequently
Auditory	You can focus on what you are hearing
● Experiential	You experience fully what is happening in the moment
Visual	You create a visual resource to review afterward

PRACTICE EXERCISE

In the first Alternate Recording Strategy box, try creating a doodle to represent the ideas in a "Fable" by Aesop.

In the second Alternate Recording Strategy box, print out and paste a photograph of a full chalkboard, whiteboard, overhead or other screenshot from a class (with your professor's permission); alternatively, take and print out a photo of notes from a classmate (again, with permission).

ALTERNATE RECORDING STRATEGY 1

Name	Date
Subject	Page

ALTERNATE RECORDING STRATEGY 2

Name	Date
Subject	Page

Review Exercise: Choosing and Developing Your Strategy

Experimenting with these strategies as part of this course will give you a sense of which one or ones may work best.

As a follow-up, try implementing your note-taking skills in another context, such as another course you are taking. Feel free to modify any of the suggested techniques from this chapter.

SECTION 2

GRAMMAR—
Working with the Building
Blocks of Communication

Many students who have grown up in North America say that although they recognize and appreciate the importance of grammar in communication, they didn't study grammar in school. Students coming up through the North American school system may recall a lot of reading, and a lot of writing—but grammar lessons?

Students were just supposed to pick up proper grammar somewhere along the way. In fact, as writing style guru William Zinsser (see Section 7) asserts, "Good writing doesn't come naturally, though most people obviously think it does."

Many North American students have learned more about grammar, its patterns, terminology, and rules, in studying Canada's official second language, French, or the second most common language in the United States, Spanish.

In order to improve our writing, we need to use the tools of grammar rather than simply saying, instinctively, "That doesn't sound right." Instead, we need to develop our own practical resources for understanding grammar in such a way as to become better writers and editors.

Students often ask how important grammar is in terms of the marking scheme for various assignments. The simple answer is that in English class, while this may not be the case for courses in other subject areas, what you say and how you say it are equally important.

In other words, you may have brilliant ideas—but if your work tends to contain numerous, significant, repeated grammatical errors, you may be very disappointed with your mark. (By the same token, if you have flawless grammar and the content of your writing doesn't meet assignment criteria, you cannot reasonably expect to get a satisfactory result).

When we write in a technological, word-processing environment, we can take advantage of identification and correction of our mistakes (although we need to be careful with these—as the unfortunate student who submitted an essay about "Canada's Unemployment Rat" would tell you), but most courses will also require you to do in-class writing, such as an essay, test, or exam.

In order to produce satisfactory work, you need to write and edit in a way that reflects proper grammar, and you need to edit your writing in order to ensure that your ideas are clear and concise. Before we get started on reviewing some of the basics of grammar, let's take this opportunity to think about the writing process itself.

Discussion and Writing Opportunity: How Can We Achieve "Clear Writing"? (Personal Reflection)

WRITING TOPICS inspired by the work of William Zinsser . . . Choose one and write three hundred words in response.

1. *"Writing is hard work. A clear sentence is no accident. Very few sentences come out right the first time, or the third. Keep thinking and rewriting until you say what you want to say."*

   How do you feel about your own writing process? Do you agree with Zinsser's statement? Use the first person ("I") to talk about your experience of writing. Do you recall a time when you had to write and rewrite to get it right?

2. *What is the importance of clear writing? Here is William Zinsser's view:*

   "The writer must therefore constantly ask himself: What am I trying to say? Surprisingly often, he doesn't know. Then he must look at what he has written and ask: Have I said it? Is it clear to someone encountering the subject for the first time?"

   Discuss your own personal view of the role of clarity in the writing process, referring to your own experiences. Was there ever a time when a lack of clarity—perhaps a grammatical mistake— resulted in a significant misunderstanding?

3. *William Zinsser claims that "the secret of good writing is to strip every sentence to its cleanest components," and he cites the work of Thoreau and Roosevelt (two of the featured writers in Section 7) as exemplary.*

   Which authors, in your life as a reader, have inspired you as providing examples of "clean" writing? What qualities do they bring to their craft? Can you think of (or find) examples of particularly powerful sentences they have written?

NOTE: Try to budget your time so that you are able to check back through what you have written to ensure that, to the best of your ability, you have edited to avoid grammatical errors that can compromise the clarity of your communication in this composition.

As a final step, add at the top an original title that reflects your choice of topic.

DISCUSSION QUESTION NUMBER	TITLE

An Overview of the Parts of Speech

Every word in every sentence you speak or write can be identified as a part of speech. Some words can be different parts of speech for different meanings (e.g., "love" = noun/verb), but a word cannot be more than one part of speech at the same time. Learning the parts of speech is important in order to understand the basic structure of sentences; these terms are also useful as diagnostic tools for identifying challenges in editing. The eight parts of speech are as follows: _nouns, pronouns, adjectives, verbs, adverbs, prepositions, conjunctions, and interjections_.

You probably know more than you realize about these eight parts of speech. See how much you recall by filling in the following self-test chart; check with a partner before you read ahead to check your results:

Part of Speech	Definition	Example

Nouns

Most students can recite the classic definition of a noun as a "person, place, or thing." A noun (or its replacement, a pronoun) can function as one of the key elements of a sentence, a subject. We also see some nouns modifying other nouns:

> _University courses_ can be challenging.

Some nouns (e.g., "concept") are _abstract_—we cannot visualize them or physically apprehend them although they are "things"; others are _concrete_—we can perceive them with our senses (e.g., "pizza").

If they are the actual names of people, institutions, publications, and so forth, we capitalize the first letter: these are _proper_ nouns. Nouns that are not capitalized are _common_ nouns—and we may need to consider the context to determine whether or not capitalization is necessary:

> Every _starship_ needs a _captain_.

> The _Starship Enterprise_ was under the command of _Captain Kirk_.

Another important distinction between types of nouns has to do with whether or not we can pluralize them. _Countable_ nouns make use of indefinite articles in the singular, and typically add "s" to create a plural:

> One _desk_, two _desks_, three _desks_ . . .

> I prefer to sit at a _desk_ when doing my work.

Uncountable (sometimes called noncount) nouns cannot be counted and do not have plurals. We can use the definite article but not the indefinite article with these nouns:

> The _information_ in our history textbook is accurate.

> I need _information_ for my report.

Some nouns are countable or uncountable depending on context:

> _Love_ is important in our lives.

> He has three _loves_: painting, music, and theater.

NOUN EXERCISE

Copy a brief paragraph from a source of your choice from our readings (see Section 7). Try to identify all of the nouns, considering the categories earlier. Double-space your work so you have plenty of room to write between the lines as necessary.

Now, make a list of all the nouns from your paragraph, and label each one: is it abstract or concrete? Common or proper? Countable or uncountable? There are other ways we can label nouns as well—feel free to do so if you find it helpful. You may use a dictionary and/ or online references to complete this exercise.

Pronouns

As you can guess from their name, pronouns ("pro" is Latin for "for") stand for, or take the place of, nouns; as such, they can function as subjects or objects in sentences. They can also denote possession.

Let's take a look at the use of pronouns in some sample sentences:

Mary is the president of the chess club at KPU.

She sets up the club's weekly meetings.

(Subjective pronoun = "she"; representing "Mary").

All the other chess players really admire *her*.

(Objective pronoun = "her"; again representing "Mary").

Other players cannot help but admire a winning strategy like *hers*.

(Possessive pronoun = "hers"; representing "Mary's").

We use the terms *first person, second person, and third person* to denote whether we are talking about the self (first), addressing someone directly (second), or referring to someone or something else (third). For each of these categories, the pronouns can be *singular* or *plural*.

I hope that *we* can work through these issues together.

(First-person pronouns = "I" [singular] and "we" [plural]; both subjective here).

You will have to decide as an individual what will benefit *you* all as a group.

(Second-person pronoun = "you" [singular and plural forms are the same; subjective and objective case also the same]).

Jo and Matti observed that the signs at the Whistler run said *it* is open, so *they* will be able to go skiing.

(Third-person pronouns = "it" [singular] and "they" [plural]; both subjective here).

Personal pronouns need to agree with their antecedents (nouns they replace) in terms of *gender*, *number*, and *case*.

In English, we have masculine, feminine, and neutral pronouns in the singular to identify the gender of the noun being replaced. Traditionally, the masculine and feminine pronouns stand for human beings, and the neutral for inanimate objects and nonhuman life forms. You will see exceptions, such as when people refer to an animal by gender. Reference to an inanimate entity such as a vehicle or a nation as female may be considered sexist.

Number has to do with singular and plural. However, since we do not have a gender-neutral singular pronoun in English, the use of the third-person plural form to denote a gender-neutral singular is increasingly standard practice.

A growing trend in many businesses and institutions is to move away from identifying human individuals by gender, and to use "they" (subjective), "them" (objective), and "their(s)" (possessive) for singular references when we do not wish to use a gendered pronoun. When writing or speaking in any academic or professional context, it is a good idea to check what the given protocols are regarding this practice.

In English, we have three cases (don't be discouraged—Latin has eight, and they affect nouns, which ours do not) that determine the form of pronouns: _subjective, objective, and possessive_. Look at the sample sentences about Mary (earlier) for an example of each of these respectively.

Reflexive pronouns have the suffixes "-self" and "-selves"; _reciprocal_ pronouns include "other"; _indefinite_ pronouns include the prefix "any-," "some-," or "no (-)"; _relative_ pronouns are "that," which," "who," "whose," "whom," "where," and "when"; _demonstrative_ pronouns are "this," "that," "these," and "those"; _interrogative_ pronouns, beginning with "wh," are used to ask a question.

Had enough of pronouns yet? Rather than studying a list of them, simply try making sure you feel comfortable using them in your own sentences.

Meanwhile, take a look at the following chart reviewing the personal pronouns, and fill it in to the best of your ability. Some spots are completed already.

PRONOUN EXERCISE

Personal Pronoun Chart: Singular Pronouns

SINGULAR	Subjective Case	Objective Case	Possessive Case
First person		Stop talking about <u>me</u>.	
Second person			The pen is <u>yours</u>.
Third person	<u>It</u> happened.		

Personal Pronoun Chart: Plural Pronouns

PLURAL	Subjective Case	Objective Case	Possessive Case
First person	<u>We</u> are ready.		
Second person		The present is for all three of <u>you</u>.	
Third person			The project is <u>theirs</u>.

NOTE: Personal pronouns do not make use of apostrophes!

Adjectives

Adjectives go with nouns, and have the function of modifying, or describing, them.

Possessive adjectives derive from pronouns, for example, "*my* car." You could go back to the pronoun chart and add possessive adjectives to the final column if you would like to review them. More than one adjective can go with the same noun, for example, "*my new* car." Commas generally do not appear before adjectives of color, for example, "*my new red* car." When we have multiple adjectives and each one separately describes the noun, we separate them with commas, for example, "*tiny, distinct, silhouetted* shapes appeared ahead as I drove my car down the highway."

We can intensify the meaning of some adjectives by using their *comparative* and *superlative* forms:

The light on the left is *brighter* than the one on the right.

(The comparative form of the adjective "bright")

The *brightest* light is the one in the middle.

(The superlative form of the adjective "bright")

Some such forms are irregular:

I was hoping for a *better* result than the one I received.

(The comparative form of the adjective "good")

The *best* things in life are free, according to an old saying.

(The superlative form of the adjective "good")

Of course, not all adjectives have these forms, and so we use "more" and "most" to intensify them.

This book is *more interesting* than I thought it would be; it may be the *most interesting* book I have read all year.

These intensified forms derive their meaning from context, and are incomplete without a frame of reference.

Advertisers sometimes deliberately use these so they can avoid contextualizing, and hope you interpret their claims in a positive way, for example, better *than other similar products*; the best *in the world*, without actually having to say so—especially if they can't prove it:

This detergent gets your clothes *cleaner*.

(Cleaner than what?)

This is the *most talented* group of performers.

(In which context?)

Some adjectives are derived from verbs (actions or states of being) and are thus "verbal."

An -ing form that has transformed into an adjective (telling what type) is called a present participial adjective. In the following sentence, find the verb:

Weird Uncle George, known affectionately as "Dracula" in our family, was terrifying the children at the party.

Now, consider the adjective in the following sentence:

That was a terrifying experience.

An -ed form (the past participle of a verb) that has transformed into an adjective is called a _past participial adjective_. In the following sentence, find the verb:

The job application required three letters of reference.

Now, find the past participial adjective in the following sentence:

The required reading for the course was a contemporary novel.

ADJECTIVE EXERCISE

Find some advertisements that make use of adjectives to sell their products or services. Put a checkmark beside the ones that seem accurate and effective, and an X beside the ones you find ambiguous or misleading. Create your own third symbol for any that you deem to be misleading yet effective.

```
AD
```

```
AD
```

AD

AD

AD

Verbs

Sentences rely on verbs for a _predicate_, to tell what happens in the sentence and to accompany the subject (whoever or whatever is doing it).

Verbs can be _transitive_ or _intransitive_ transitive verbs take a direct object (no preposition comes between the verb and its object); intransitive verbs take an indirect object (a preposition is required between the verb and its object):

TRANSITIVE: I opened the door.

INTRANSITIVE: She talks to her mother every day.

Voice can be _active_ or _passive_: in the active voice, which George Orwell advocates in "Politics and the English Language," the subject performs the action; in the passive voice, the subject receives the action:

ACTIVE: Deborah kicked the dog.

PASSIVE: The dog was kicked by Deborah.

Mood can be _imperative_ (command: "Do it!"), _interrogative_ (question: "Will you?"), _indicative_ (statement: "I will . . ."), _conditional_ (possibility: "I would reconsider"), or _subjunctive_ (hypothesis: "if I were you").

Verbs have three "principal parts": _bare infinitive, past tense, past participle_. These can be _regular_ (past tense and past participle are formed by adding "ed" to the bare infinitive) or _irregular_ (past tense and past participle are formed otherwise). A dictionary will tell you whether the verb you are looking up is of the former or the latter classification.

Bare Infinitive	Past Tense	Past Participle
Regular verb: walk	walked	walked
Irregular verb: write	wrote	written

To make a _perfect_ tense, use a form of the verb "to have" plus a past participle. To make a _progressive_ tense, use a form of the verb "to be" plus a present participle (i.e., the "ing" form of the verb).

NOTE: A _modal_ is an auxiliary verb that expresses necessity or possibility. English modal verbs include _must, shall, will, should, would, can, could, may_, and _might_.

VERB TENSE CHART

Tense	Example	Meaning
Simple present	I take the bus to work.	— states a fact or indicates a habit
Present progressive	I am studying Egyptian art.	— emphasizes process or continuation/what is happening now
Present perfect	I have studied at UBC for three years.	— connects a beginning in the past to the reality of the present
Present perfect progressive	I have been hoping to go to Paris.	— emphasizes a beginning in the past, a connection to present reality, and a sense of process or continuation
Simple past	He broke her heart.	— indicates it is over
Past progressive	He was dating other women.	— is a process or continuation of past action
Past perfect	He had promised to be faithful.	— shows action further past than other past action
Past perfect progressive	They had been planning to go to Disney World.	— emphasizes process of a past action prior to another past action
Simple future	The students will write the test later.	— indicates certainty of what is ahead
Future progressive	My parents will be visiting me next summer.	— emphasizes future process or continuation
Future perfect	She will have been at UBC for four years by the time she graduates.	— indicates something that will be true or complete in the future
Future perfect progressive	She will have been studying for eight years to be an MD by 2028.	— emphasizes process of something that will be true or complete in future

VERB EXERCISE

Tense	Verb Form	Sample Sentence
Simple present		
Present progressive		
Present perfect		
Present perfect progressive		
Simple past		
Past progressive		
Past perfect		
Past perfect progressive		
Simple future		
Future progressive		
Future perfect		
Future perfect progressive		

Now, try writing a short paragraph that makes use of a selection of these tenses. Remember, you will need transitions, for example, "I hated pizza when I was a child, but I love it now."

Adverbs

One common grammatical error is to mix up adverbs with adjectives; you can avoid this pitfall by understanding their different functions.

One "rule" students sometimes tell me they learned in the past is that adverbs, unlike adjectives, end in "-ly," and we can change adjectives to adverbs by adding "-ly" accordingly. This rule does work some of the time:

ADJECTIVE:
The group's _quick_ response to the question impressed their classmates.

ADVERB:
Jordan ran _quickly_ down the stairs.

However, a number of words ending in "-ly" are not adjectives; consider the adjectives "silly" and "friendly," for example. And not all adverbs end in "-ly," as you will see in the following sentences.

Adverbs have a variety of distinct uses: we use them for modification of verbs, adjectives, and (other) adverbs.

Whereas adjectives often answer the question, "What Type?" adverbs can answer the question, "How?" Think of the question, "How?" in each instance:

Jessie _correctly_ completed all parts of the assignment.

(How did Jessie complete the assignment? Correctly).

The group _very effectively_ handled the questions from their audience.

(How effectively did they handle the questions? Very effectively).

The whole class was _very_ impressed by the presentation.

(How impressed was the class? Very impressed).

ADVERB CHART

The following, divided into three useful categories, are just some of the many, many adverbs available to us as writers. Note that some are adverb phrases, that is, made up of two or more words that go together to create the meaning. Also, note that not all end in "-ly"! There is room in each section to add your own selections to the chart if you wish.

"How?" Adverbs	"How Much?" Adverbs	"How Often" Adverbs	Conjunctive Adverbs (Transitions)
— carefully	— very	— usually	— however
— slowly	— extremely	— regularly	— moreover
— quickly	— overwhelmingly	— frequently	— in addition
— happily	— really	— often	— on the other hand
— joyfully	— not really	— rarely	— unfortunately
— cheerfully	— totally	— never	— fortunately
— sadly	— completely	— daily	— indeed
— mournfully	— partially	— weekly	— contrastingly
— badly	— somewhat	— monthly	—
— laughably	— barely	— annually	
— ridiculously	—	—	
—			

ADVERB EXERCISE

Try creating sentences that make use of adverbs that have the distinct functions of modifying verbs, adjectives, and other adverbs; try writing or finding in others' writing three of each type, and avoid using the adverbs in the sentences earlier ("quickly," "correctly," "effectively, "very").

Now, think of a particular process or set of instructions, in which you are telling someone how to do something, perhaps through a series of steps or instructions; as you do so, think of adding in adverbs that will clarify the technique. Underline or highlight the adverbs you have chosen to use.

HOW TO_____

Conjunctions

Conjunctions are joining words; they join parts of sentences together.

If you look closely at the term, you will see the word "junction," the same word we use to mean a joining place in a road or railway.

If one part is lesser in importance than the other, we use a _subordinating conjunction_. The part with the subordinating conjunction cannot stand on its own as a sentence:

> Rory was late _because_ the busses were off schedule in the bad weather.

If we are joining parts of equal value, we use a _coordinating conjunction_.

> The weather was bad, <u>so</u> the busses were running late.

The only coordinating conjunction that requires special attention in terms of word order in the sentence is "nor." When we use "nor," we need to separate the two parts of the verb, and we need to put the subject after the first part.

> The busses did not go at their usual speed, nor did they run as frequently.

> Traveling on public transit is not always easy, nor is it always reliable.

In our discussion of Sentence Structure (later in this chapter), we will cover the different punctuation requirements for sentences making use of coordinating and subordinating conjunctions.

We can also consider _correlative conjunctions_, pairs such as "both/and," "either/or," "neither/nor," "not/but," and "not only/but also."

A related category is that of _conjunctive adverbs_, which you may know already as transitions (e.g., "however," "moreover," "nonetheless"). These are adverbs that have a joining role, and we often see them in academic writing.

The principal value of using conjunctions is in showing the relation between ideas; indeed, it would be virtually impossible to write an advanced-level composition without them.

CONJUNCTION CHART

Note that for the coordinating conjunctions (the ones that join equal parts of sentences), we have only seven: the FANBOYS. The subordinating conjunctions are too numerous for a quick mnemonic list. Some common ones are listed here, and there is room in the chart for you to add more.

Coordinating Conjunctions	Subordinating Conjunctions
— for	— because
— and	— while
— nor	— since
— but	— after
— or	— when
— yet	— if
— so	— although
(no others)	— even though
	— as
	—

CONJUNCTION EXERCISE

Fill in the missing coordinating conjunctions in the first column, and make up your own story using the "FANBOYS."

Coordinating Conjunctions (The "Fanboys")	Meaning	Example	Your Story
	Causality (because)	Emily could not forgive John, for he had broken her heart.	
	Addition (moreover)	John had forgotten Emily's cat's birthday, and he did not appear to be sorry.	
	Additional negative (neither)	Emily would not pick up the phone when John called, nor would she answer his e-mails.	
	Contrast (however)	He begged for her forgiveness, but she refused to speak to him.	

Coordinating Conjunctions (The "Fanboys")	Meaning	Example	Your Story
	Other possible option (alternatively)	Would they get back together, or were they doomed to lives of loneliness?	
	Persistence/ contrast (still)	She could not forgive him, yet she could not live without him.	
	Result (thus)	They could not live apart, so they got back together.	

Prepositions

Just as we see the word "junction" in "conjunction," we can see the word "position" in "preposition." Prepositions can indicate position in a physical sense, or in a more abstract way:

> Lesley entered _through_ the front door.

> We can understand grammar _through_ studying these materials.

Sometimes we can figure out which preposition to use by thinking about the meaning in terms of physical position:

> The butter is _in_ the refrigerator.

> The bread is _on_ the counter.

However, the process is not always so straightforward. The use of prepositions is governed by _idiom_—that is, by standard patterns that sound right to native speakers of a language.

> I'm _in_ the car.

> I'm _on_ the bus.

You may need to commit to memory, especially if you speak English as an additional language, which prepositions go with certain nouns and verbs.

You will get used to idiomatic expressions—but it may take a while, so be patient with yourself, and ask for help from native speakers when you can.

It's also true that some slang patterns may sound idiomatic even to native speakers and yet be inappropriate for formal writing contexts. For example, your friends may tell you they are "excited to" do something or go somewhere; the proper idiom is "excited about" doing or going, and so forth.

In the following exercise, several prepositions are listed.

Prepositions can be more than a single word, as when they are _double_ (two prepositions combined for a new meaning) or _compound_ (with other words as well). Here is a chart containing some of these; there is extra space for you to add your own examples if you wish.

Double Preps	Compound Preps
— into	— in addition to
— onto	— on behalf of
— within	— in the midst of
— atop	— according to
— upon	— with respect to
— up to	— in relation to
— out of	— by means of
— without	— in order to
— throughout	— for the purposes of
— off to	— in accordance with
— at about	— in terms of
— at around	— on the basis of
	— with a view to

PREPOSITION EXERCISE

Write one sentence for each of the following prepositions:

In	
to	
on	
from	
at	
with	
through	

after	
of———————————	
between	
by	
across	

Now, try some of your own examples from the chart containing double and compound prepositions:

Interjections

When we interject, we are exclaiming in a way that announces the unexpected and expresses surprise or another sudden emotion such as dismay or pleasure. We use interjections (of one word or more) frequently in everyday conversation, often preceding a dramatic statement and standing alone, followed by an exclamation mark:

Wow! That's a great haircut.

Hey! If you don't slow down, you're going to do some damage.

Good grief! I can't believe you are dating him again.

While we see interjections frequently in dialog, they are much less common in professional and academic documents, in many cases due to their lack of formality.

Here are some contexts in which we might use interjections, as in casual conversation. Feel free to add your own examples to the chart:

Surprise	Greeting	Agreement
— yikes	— hey	— sure
— wow	— hi	— OK
— aha	— hello	— yeah
— oh	— yo	— aye
— whoa	— cheers	— uh-huh
—	—	—

A few interjections are rather more sophisticated than the ones earlier, and we might expect to see them in a formal sophisticated context:

Alas, these findings were inconclusive.

Note that in such formal contexts, we should use them with commas rather than as exclamations. In general, we might say that academic and professional documents are objective accounts, in which a subjective and emotional response may be out of place.

Be especially careful not to use interjections that your reader or listener may find offensive due to profanity or vulgarity. As well, be aware that interjections are idiomatic—you can't make up your own (unless perhaps for comic effect—always a risk).

Here are some suggestions for replacing informal interjections; add your own examples if you wish.

Informal Interjection	More Formal Substitute
— Yeah, sure.	— I agree (e.g., in a business meeting)
— Wait! What!?	— That is truly surprising (e.g., a response to information in a document from a colleague)
— Yo! Hey!	— Greetings and welcome (e.g., at a formal event)
—	—

In order to prepare for the following exercise, read through any piece (or pieces) of writing containing dialog, such as a short story, an interview, even a graphic novel. List as many interjections as you can find, and write down the associated meanings, for example, "Gadzooks!" (response as a character in a short story jumps out from behind a curtain)—shock at the unexpected, perhaps some fear. If you are not sure about what the interjection is intended to convey, write "not sure" or "don't know" in the second column—but try to at least guess from context.

INTERJECTION EXERCISE

Interjection in Context	Meaning

NOTE: Feel free to include more formal examples from professional or academic documents if you wish.

PARTS OF SPEECH COMPREHENSIVE REVIEW CHART

	Notes, Examples
NOUNS	
PRONOUNS	
ADJECTIVES	
VERBS	
ADVERBS	
CONJUNCTIONS	
PREPOSITIONS	
INTERJECTIONS	

An Overview of Sentence Structure

Phrases

Phrases are groups of words that, although they do not contain a subject–verb combination, go together syntactically to create meaning; with a basic understanding of the parts of speech, we can see how certain types of phrases work.

NOUN PHRASE: Raj transferred to *the University of British Columbia*.

In this sentence, the noun phrase is the object of the preposition "to."

Try writing your own example; highlight, circle, or underline the phrase:

_____

ADJECTIVE PHRASE: Jo purchased *the least expensive* coat available.

In this sentence, the adjective phrase modifies the noun "coat."

Try writing your own example; highlight, circle, or underline the phrase:

_____

ADVERB PHRASE: Please return my book *whenever possible*.

In this sentence, the adverb phrase modifies the verb "return."

Try writing your own example; highlight, circle, or underline the phrase:

_____

VERB PHRASE: Lachlan *has been waking up* early lately.

In this sentence, the verb phrase is the predicate of the sentence.

Try writing your own example; highlight, circle, or underline the phrase:

_____

→ NOTE: A PHRASE ON ITS OWN CANNOT BE A COMPLETE SENTENCE (it is a fragment without a subject–verb combination).

Clauses

Clauses contain subjects and verbs, and can serve a variety of functions (as earlier); with a subordinating conjunction, a clause is _dependent_ (or _subordinate_); if _independent_ (without a subordinating conjunction), this type of clause (also called a _main_ clause) can stand alone as a sentence.

INDEPENDENT/MAIN CLAUSE: _I like bananas_.

This clause can stand on its own as a complete (simple) sentence; we will look at types of sentences in the next section of the text.

Try writing your own example of an independent clause:

_____

DEPENDENT/SUBORDINATE CLAUSE: _Because I like bananas_ ... This clause cannot stand on its own as a sentence; we would need to put an independent clause before or after it to avoid a sentence fragment.

Try writing your own example of a dependent clause with a subordinating conjunction:

_____

→ NOTE: AN INDEPENDENT CLAUSE CAN FUNCTION AS A COMPLETE SENTENCE; A DEPENDENT CLAUSE CANNOT DO SO (each sentence requires at least one independent clause).

Now, add an independent clause to the beginning or end of your dependent clause. If you put the independent clause first, you won't need a comma; if you put the dependent clause first, you will need to put a comma before the independent clause:

Our family will go to Vancouver Island after we meet up with our friends.

After we meet up with our friends, our family will go to Vancouver Island.

Grammatical Types of Sentence Structures: Simple, Compound, Complex, and Compound-Complex

Your sentences should reflect a variety of structures.

1. SIMPLE (one independent clause)

   <u>My dog ate my homework</u>.

   Independent (main) clause ending with a period, question mark, or exclamation

2. COMPOUND (two independent clauses)

   <u>My dog ate my homework</u>; <u>he was very hungry</u>.

   Independent clause + semicolon + independent clause

   <u>My dog ate my homework</u>; <u>evidently, he was very hungry</u>.

   Independent clause + semicolon + conjunctive adverb + independent clause

   <u>My dog ate my homework</u>, <u>so I am unable to hand it in today</u>.

   Independent clause + comma + coordinating conjunction + independent clause

3. COMPLEX (an independent and a dependent clause)

   <u>I am unable to hand in my homework today because my dog ate it</u>.

   Independent clause + dependent clause

   <u>Since my dog ate my homework</u>, <u>I am unable to hand it in today</u>.

   Dependent clause + comma + independent clause

4. COMPOUND-COMPLEX (at least two independent clauses + one dependent clause, in any order).

   <u>Since my dog ate my homework</u>, <u>I am unable to hand it in today</u>; <u>evidently, he was very hungry</u>.

Stylistic Types of Sentence Structures: Loose, Periodic, and Balanced

We can also classify sentences in terms of their stylistic types: _loose_, _periodic_, and _balanced_.

These are not mutually exclusive with the grammatical types, that is, a sentence can be simple and loose, simple and periodic, and so forth. Any type of sentence can also be balanced.

By using a variety of stylistic sentence types in your writing, you can add to its appeal and effectiveness.

Here are the basic definitions of each type, with examples:

A. LOOSE (begins with subject)

I am unable to hand in my homework today.

B. PERIODIC (begins with introductory word, phrase, or subordinate clause + comma)

Evidently, my dog was very hungry.

In the blink of an eye, my homework disappeared.

Since my dog ate my homework, I am unable to hand it in today.

C. BALANCED (strategic use of repetition/parallel elements)

Eating, sleeping, playing, and watching television are my dog's favorite activities.

He eats; he sleeps; he plays; he watches television.

Sometimes, when he eats, he eats my homework.

NOTE: If you listen to political speeches, you will frequently hear balanced structures, as they serve to reinforce ideas in an emphatic way.

SENTENCE VARIETY EXERCISE

Write your own examples of the various types of sentences.

Grammatical Type	Example
SIMPLE	
COMPOUND	
COMPLEX	
COMPOUND-COMPLEX	

Stylistic Type	Example
LOOSE	
PERIODIC	
BALANCED	

Now, find a short paragraph from one of our readings and label the sentences according to type.

Common Errors: Fragments, Run-Ons, Dangling and Misplaced Modifiers, Mixed Constructions

DIAGNOSING AND FIXING SENTENCE STRUCTURE ERRORS

Types of fragments:

1. Subordinate clause (subordinating conjunction + subject + verb)

   For example, I shop at a store called Bananas R Us. *Because I like bananas.* X

2. Phrase or single word

   For example, What should we pack for snacks on our trip? *Bananas.* X

   When should we leave? *In an hour.* X

Types of run-ons:

1. Fused sentences (two independent clauses with no punctuation between them)

   For example, *I like him he's nice.* X

2. Comma splices

   For example, *I like him, he's nice.* X

   (Sometimes permissible if clauses are short and sweet—but usually best not to risk!)

3. Inadequate punctuation and/or cumbersome structure (missing punctuation marks, too many stacked phrases/clauses, etc.)

I can't bear to make up an example for this one but I'm sure you know what I mean, some people talk like this or even worse think like this and that is really quite frightening or some would say confusing or some would say just plain annoying and yet with just a little attention to it, we could solve the problem easily and it's amazing to me that more people aren't aware of this problem and how to fix it . . . X

SENTENCE STRUCTURE EXERCISE

When you have a phrase before a comma preceding the subject of a periodic sentence, that group of words is understood to modify that subject. If it doesn't, you have a _dangling modifier_ error. These errors are quite common, so you will see them—and hear them—all around you! So, what's the mental picture you get when you read the following sentences? You can even draw the picture if you like! Then think about how you could recraft the sentences to clarify the meaning.

Barking loudly, Deborah restrained her dog.

_____

Walking across campus last night, the tall buildings looked frightening.

_____

Scratching each other playfully, we watched the monkeys at the zoo.

_____

Crispy and delicious, your kids will love our restaurant's new recipe.

_____

Delightfully frosted and decorated with sprinkles and tiny edible ornaments, the pastry chef was proud of her award-winning cake.

_____

Modifiers that do not clearly go with a particular noun are _misplaced_ or _squinting_.

You should never eat a raspberry jam tart _wearing a white shirt_.

_____

Jared _almost_ ate the entire cake.

_____

Essentials of Punctuation

Punctuation allows us to understand how ideas fit together. If we get it wrong, we may change the meaning of our sentences entirely.

Consider the difference between these two sentences:

> Let's eat, dog.

> Let's eat dog.

Find your own examples of punctuation pitfalls!

Punctuation contains clues about how we speak, such as pausing between ideas and modulating our tone of voice (e.g., when we ask a question, our tone of voice goes up at the end). Even if we are not speaking aloud, we still use punctuation visually to understand the meaning of what we read.

In this section of the text, we will consider the following punctuation marks:

What It's Called	What It Looks Like
Period	.
Ellipsis	. . .
Comma	,
Semicolon	;
Colon	:
Exclamation	!
Dash	—
Quotation	"
Apostrophe	'
Question	?

Period and Ellipsis

A period, also called a full stop, ends sentences (unless they are direct questions or exclamations). The period is thus a visual clue that an idea is complete. Another visual clue for us as readers is that a capital letter begins the next sentence.

While periods and capital letters may be disappearing from text messages in today's communication (some people don't use periods in texts because they feel that a full stop conveys harshness or abruptness—even rudeness!), they are absolutely essential for clarity in academic and professional documents.

If you use mostly short, simple sentences, you may see many periods in your writing—perhaps too many. Short, choppy sentences can lead to a simplistic, abrupt sounding document. For coherence and appeal, a variety of sentence structures should characterize your projects, essays, reports—even e-mails.

In informal contexts, especially when we are not sure how to end what we are saying, or don't want to convey the sense of an abrupt ending with a single period, we may use ellipses (colloquially known as dot-dot-dot), as in "See you later . . ."

However, we should not use ellipsis in this casual way when we are writing in an academic or professional context. The proper use of ellipsis (plural = ellipses) is to replace missing material from a quoted passage.

When we remove the words we wish to leave out, we need to ensure that the basic meaning and the sentence structure are intact.

To give an extreme example, imagine that the missing words are "not at all" in an original sentence, "The company was not at all happy with the results." Equally important is the structural integrity—we cannot simply put in the beginning ("The company") followed by ellipses and the ending ("results").

When we use ellipses, we need to consider the fact that the reader probably does not have access to the original document from which we are quoting; our audience relies on us to give enough information from the passage to coherently relay the gist of the ideas.

Find or create examples of formal and informal writing situations in which periods and ellipses appear. Feel free to look at advertisements, news articles, popular magazines, comics, and so forth.

PERIOD AND ELLIPSIS EXERCISE

Find or create examples of formal and informal writing situations in which periods and ellipses appear. Feel free to look at advertisements, news articles, popular magazines, comics, and so forth (or should I say, "dot-dot-dot" . . .)

Formal Use	Informal Use

Now, trying using ellipses to quote from some of Section 7; put the author's last name and page number in parentheses afterward.

Comma

The most common rule students tell me they have learned is to insert a comma "wherever you would pause for breath." While this strategy may work in some situations, it is not always the rule to follow. Imagine the following couple of sentences:

Darien is one of the most talented and popular visual artists in BC.

Darien's siblings have no interest in art.

If I were saying those two sentences consecutively aloud, I might well pause after saying "Darien's siblings" for emphasis. However, it would be incorrect to place a comma between "siblings" and "have" in that sentence.

When we add in extra information, that is, _parenthetical elements_ or _appositives_ in the sentence, we can use commas (or dashes) to surround that material (commas connote additional ideas, while dashes connote surprising additional ideas):

Darien's siblings, who are all engineers, have no interest in art.

Try writing your own example with commas surrounding parenthetical elements:

_____

We can tell that the information is parenthetical because when we remove it, the basic idea of the sentence still makes sense.

Another use of the comma is to separate items in a list:

Darien's siblings, parents, and grandparents are all scientists.

Try writing your own example with commas separating items in a list:

_____

The comma before the last item (sometimes called "the Oxford comma" is optional).

If you decide to eliminate the comma before the final list item, watch out for ambiguities that can arise when we are not sure whether the last two items are to be understood as separate items. Consider the difference between the following sentences:

The grocery list is clear: bananas, bread, butter, macaroni, and cheese.

The grocery list is clear: bananas, bread, butter, macaroni and cheese.

We can also use the comma after an introductory element (word, phrase, or subordinate clause) in a periodic sentence.

Unfortunately, Darien's siblings have no interest in art.

Your own example:

_____

_____

In a family of engineers, Darien is the only artist.

Your own example:

_____

_____

Although they have no interest in art, Darien's siblings are supportive.

Your own example:

_____

_____

A comma can also be used to separate two independent clauses joined by a coordinating conjunction:

Darien loves art, but his parents and siblings have no interest in it.

Your own example:

_____

_____

COMMA EXERCISE

In Section 7, try finding sentences that use commas in the following ways:

Use of Comma	Examples
SURROUNDING AN APPOSITIVE	
IN A LIST	
AFTER AN INTRODUCTORY WORD	
AFTER AN INTRODUCTORY PHRASE	
AFTER A SUBORDINATE CLAUSE	
IN A COMPOUND SENTENCE WITH A COORDINATING CONJUNCTION	

"[Our] power to connect his thought with its proper symbol, and so to utter it, depends on ... simplicity ...[,] love of truth, and ... desire to communicate it without loss. The corruption of [humanity] is followed by the corruption of language. When simplicity of character and the sovereignty of ideas is broken up by the prevalence of secondary desires, the desire of riches, of pleasure, of power, and of praise, — and duplicity and falsehood take place of simplicity and truth, the power over nature as an interpreter of the will, is in a degree lost; new imagery ceases to be created, and old words are perverted to stand for things which are not ...

—*Ralph Waldo Emerson, "Language"*

Semicolon

As we saw in the section on Sentence Types, understanding sentence structures can give us a good idea of how to use punctuation properly. For instance, the difference between commas and semicolons is clear: a comma alone should not separate two independent clauses.

A semicolon alone can separate two independent clauses if the relationship between the two ideas is evident and requires no further clarification:

I like Vancouver; it's a great city.

These two ideas are clearly related, and we do not require anything beyond the semicolon to show the relationship between them because it is natural to like people who are nice. Consider this next sentence:

I like Vancouver; the weather is rainy most of the time.

Now the relationship between ideas is not clear; no inherent connection exists between liking a city and rainy weather. If the previous sentence sets up a logical progression of ideas, we could use a transition and a comma after the semicolon to clarify the meaning. Try it:

_____

_____

We also use semicolons in complicated lists (usually preceded by a colon), in which the list items themselves already contain commas.

We visited three cities: Kingston, Ontario; Edmonton, Alberta; and Regina, Saskatchewan. Let me introduce our research team: Gloria, our leader; George, her assistant; and Jules, their secretary.

Try it:

_____

_____

While you will have more than one semicolon in a complicated list of this type, a compound sentence will usually contain a maximum of one semicolon.

Colon

A full colon, which precedes explanatory material or examples, is a punctuation mark we often see in academic writing. This makes sense when we consider that academic writing often includes such explanations.

Students often ask about the difference between a colon (sometimes called a full colon) and a semicolon. In terms of the ideas in the sentence, a semicolon separates related, equal ideas; a full colon shows that one part of the sentence explains the other. Grammatically, the difference is that a semicolon separates independent clauses, whereas a colon requires only one independent clause either beforehand or afterward (although it is also possible to have both parts as independent clauses).

Each option conveys a unique emphasis; all are correct.

> He has one fear: he is terrified of bats.

> He has one fear: bats.

> A terror of bats: this is his one fear.

Sometimes students tell me that they have learned that a colon should go before any list; however, that is not always the case.

Where we have a complicated list, a colon works well after an independent clause that works as a complete sentence.

> We visited three cities: Kingston, Ontario; Edmonton, Alberta; and Regina, Saskatchewan.

Note that we would not want to delete "three cities" if we want to use this pattern; we want the first part of the sentence to work well as a complete sentence unit.

Now consider a simple list; we would not want to insert a colon between the verb and list of its objects:

> I went to the store to buy apples, oranges, and bananas.

If we do want to use a colon in such a situation, we need to expand the first part, such as by adding "the following items," so it could be a complete sentence unit on its own.

COLON AND SEMICOLON EXERCISE

Practice using semicolons according to these patterns.

SEMICOLON SEPARATING INDEPENDENT CLAUSES

SEMICOLON + CONJUNCTIVE ADVERB + COMMA SEPARATING INDEPENDENT CLAUSES

SEMICOLONS IN A COMPLICATED LIST INTRODUCED BY A COLON

COLON SEPARATING INDEPENDENT CLAUSES (SECOND CLAUSE EXPLAINS THE FIRST)

COLON FOLLOWS INDEPENDENT CLAUSE (SECOND PART OF SENTENCE IS AN EXPLANATORY WORD OR PHRASE)

COLON AFTER INDEPENDENT CLAUSE INTRODUCES A LIST WITH COMMAS

Words are signs of natural facts....Every word which is used to express a moral or intellectual fact, if traced to its root, is found to be borrowed from some material appearance....Most of the process by which this transformation is made, is hidden from us in the remote time when language was framed; but the same tendency may be daily observed in children....But this origin of all words that convey a spiritual import, — so conspicuous a fact in the history of language, — is our least debt to nature. It is not words only that are emblematic; it is things which are emblematic. Every natural fact is a symbol of some spiritual fact. Every appearance in nature corresponds to some state of the mind, and that state of the mind can only be described by presenting that natural appearance as its picture.

—*Ralph Waldo Emerson, "Language"*

Dash

Traditionally, the dash was an informal punctuation mark that rarely found its way into professional communications, but it has really come into its own now as a versatile and meaningful way to show emphasis in writing.

When you use the dash, be sure you do require specific emphasis, as that is the effect you will achieve. Overuse of the dash creates a visual distraction in the document, so judge carefully. More than a few would probably be too many!

Note the typographic difference between a dash and a hyphen. A hyphen divides compound words such as self-confidence. To create a dash in typography, either type a word + no space + two hyphens + no space + next word. Another option is to type a word + a space + a hyphen + a space.

The first option earlier—by far the most popular—is my own personal preference.

The second option - which you are free to choose - is also acceptable.

To insert parenthetical elements into the middle of a sentence, make sure you have both dashes. Alternatively, you can put the extra material at the end of the sentence—if you wish to end with the point you are emphasizing. Rarer still—you can put it at the beginning.

Sometimes the dash can save your bacon grammatically—if you are unsure as to which punctuation mark you need. In the previous sentence, no punctuation is required—but the dash creates emphasis. In the second sentence in this paragraph—the one preceding this one—a comma is required, but a dash is also correct.

Those parenthetical dashes can replace either commas or parentheses—even a semicolon, a full colon, or a period can be a dash instead (as long as what follows makes sense grammatically). Variant sentence structures do reflect differing emphases, so you can make your own stylistic choice: to use—or not to use—the dash.

The _em dash_ is the standard dash. An _en dash_ is longer than a hyphen but shorter than an em dash, and is typically used for ranges of numbers and dates, as well as in complex compound adjectives, for example, "an e-book-only publisher."

Exclamation

Exclamation marks (also called exclamation points) are rare in formal writing; like interjections, they express subjective emotion at odds with the objectivity of professional and academic documents.

Other than to convey emotion, we also tend to use exclamation marks to add emphasis or forcefulness to what we say. That is not to say that we want to avoid being forceful or emphatic.

In formal writing, the challenge is to use word choice, word order, and sentence structure to achieve the desired effect.

If you find yourself wanting to use an exclamation mark, try rewording and reordering your sentence in such a way as to create the emphasis you have in mind.

Here is an example of an original sentence that contains an exclamation mark:

My mother ran a marathon at age 63!

By altering the structure of the sentence, we can clarify which part of the information is surprising:

At age 63, my mother ran a marathon.

My mother—at age 63—ran a marathon.

Alternatively, we could add an introductory element to show more about how this information is surprising:

Impressively, my mother ran a marathon at age 63.

Never double (or triple or more) an exclamation mark or combine it with a question mark in formal writing; not only does it look unprofessional, but it may convey a sense of anger or impatience (whether or not that is your intent, especially when communicating with an academic or professional contact, for example, in an e-mail to a professor, "I stopped by your office, but you were not there!?!")

In short, the best ways to achieve emphasis in formal writing are through strategic use of sentence structure (word order) and diction (word choice).

EMPHASIS EXERCISE

Read the following variations and create your own examples, using different ideas:

DASH SEPARATING INDEPENDENT CLAUSES

He has one fear—he is terrified of bats.

_____

_____

DASH BEFORE CONCLUDING ELEMENTS IN THE SENTENCE (word, phrase, subordinate clause)

He has one fear—bats.

_____

Only one factor prevented him from exploring caves on his vacation—a fear of bats.

_____

He feels fear in only one situation—whenever he sees bats.

_____

DASHES SURROUNDING PARENTHETICAL ELEMENTS IN THE SENTENCE

Bats—his only fear—strike terror into his heart.

_____

Now, complete the following chart, using examples from reading materials or from your own imagination.

EXCLAMATORY REMARK WITH !	REPHRASING FOR EMPHASIS

Quotation

Note that quotation mark protocols are not the same universally (e.g., the United Kingdom uses different rules), and that the following guidelines are traditional to the MLA (Modern Language Association) style, which is a North American institution. As such, the default usage of quotation marks is double quotes, with single quotes within doubles as needed (for quotes within quotes).

"He didn't call me 'Honeybunch' the whole time we were married," she cried.

We use quotations for both spoken and written words that are direct quotes.

"I wonder if he's going out with others now that we've split up," she mused.

She wondered if he had begun dating since their marriage had ended.

"Please accept this token of my esteem, and read it for inspiration and comfort," said the note accompanying his Christmas gift to her, <u>The Holy Bible</u> (King James Version).

"It's a good thing I read the part about 'Thou shalt not kill,'" she grumbled.

We also use quotes for song, poem, and story titles (not books, journals, movies).

"I Got You, Babe" used to be their favorite song. She even made a JibJab video of it once for Valentine's Day.

We can use square brackets to alter quotations, putting the part we have changed into the parentheses. If we want to leave the quote intact, with nonstandard usage, we use (sic) to show "it was written thus" ("sic" means "thus" in Latin).

She doesn't certainly doesn't "got" him anymore (sic), nor does she want to "hold [his] hand," "wear [his] ring," or do any of the romantic activities mentioned in the song originally performed by Sonny and Cher.

If we have a longer, indented (ten spaces on the left side) quotation, we do not use quotation marks.

> You once gave me a rose so red,
>
> But now I frankly wish you dead;
>
> Good luck with all your Facebook friends,
>
> For this is where our marriage ends.

Apostrophe

The apostrophe, which you type the same way you would a single quote, inspires fear and loathing in many amateur writers—some linguists predict the apostrophe will pass out of English all together—but that need not be so! Here are the standard uses:

CONTRACTIONS (note, we do not typically use these in formal writing situations)

> He should've tried . . .

POSSESSIVE NOUNS (NOT PRONOUNS, e.g., its, hers, yours, theirs, ours):

> The cat's toy . . .
>
> John's book . . .
>
> KPU's policies . . .

FAQs about apostrophes:

→ After numbers and acronyms to show pluralization? This issue is somewhat controversial, but the traditional answer is NO.

> The 1930s were a turbulent era.
>
> My brother collected 750 CDs before they became obsolete.

→ What if the noun is plural AND possessive? The apostrophe goes after the s.

> My friends' hobbies are expensive.

→ What if the noun is not plural, but ends in s? You will typically need s + apostrophe + s, though some linguists advocate following verbal patterns as spoken aloud.

> The truss's strength determines the viability of the structure.
>
> For goodness' sake!

→ What about proper nouns ending in s? Variations depend on idiom, again reflecting speech patterns . . .

> The Stones' concert showcased the iconic group's geriatric performers.
>
> Chris's essay was the best in the class.

QUOTATION AND APOSTROPHE EXERCISE

Complete the following chart with your own examples.

Use of Quotes	Example
DIRECT SPEECH	
QUOTES WITHIN QUOTES	
SONG	
POEM	
STORY	
ALTERED QUOTATION	
INDENTED QUOTATION	

Complete the following chart with your own examples.

Use of Apostrophe	Example
CONTRACTION	
POSSESSION (SINGULAR)	
POSSESSION (PLURAL)	
POSSESSION (SINGULAR NOUN ENDING IN S)	
POSSESSION (SINGULAR PROPER NOUN ENDING IN S)	
POSSESSION (PLURAL PROPER NOUN ENDING IN S)	
NO APOSTROPHE!	

Question Mark

Asking a question can be a very effective way to spark your audience's attention and to make them think about the subject you are discussing.

If you are in a writing or speaking situation in which you cannot expect an answer in return, this is called a rhetorical question.

Use rhetorical questions sparingly—too many may be distracting or annoying to the reader. Some instructors may suggest a limit of one per essay, or at most one per paragraph.

Also, make sure, if you use a question mark, that you are actually asking a direct question.

DIRECT QUESTIONS (use a question mark):

Will it rain tomorrow?

Are these results conclusive?

What will the global environment look like one hundred years from now?

INDIRECT QUESTIONS (do not use a question mark):

I wonder if it will rain tomorrow.

We need to determine whether or not these results are conclusive.

No one knows what the global environment will look like one hundred years from now.

Note the word order in the direct question format, whereby the verb is in two parts and the subject is situated between them. This is not the case for the indirect question structure.

If you do ask a direct question and provide the answer, make sure you do so in a complete sentence (as opposed to a single word, such as "Maybe" or "Uncertain," or a sentence fragment, such as "Not possible to predict," if you are in a formal writing situation).

In many situations, you may find that an indirect question is a suitable alternative to the direct question you were thinking of asking.

A common enquiry from students is whether or not to put a question mark inside quotation marks. The answer depends on context. If the question is part of what is being said, we do put the question inside the quotation marks (and we do not put a period afterward):

Students often ask, "Do question mark go inside quotes?"

Your own example:

_____

_____

If the quoted material is part of a larger question that the quotation is in, we put the question mark outside the quotation marks:

In formal academic writing, should we refer to "quotations" rather than "quotes"?

Your own example:

_____

_____

Observe what happens in situations where we have single quotes within doubles:

Students often ask, "In formal academic writing, should we refer to 'quotations' rather than 'quotes'?"

Your own example:

_____

_____

QUESTION MARK EXERCISE

Put a star beside which version is the original (from selected Readings or your own creation); then complete the other column in the chart.

Direct Question	Indirect Question

Review Exercise: A Comprehensive Grammar Inventory

On your own or with a partner, look through your own writing from this course (or others) and find ten sentences with grammatical errors requiring editing. Try to diagnose the issue (whether or not the error has been labeled when marked), and correct it.

Original Error	Diagnosis	Revision

SECTION 3

COMPOSITION STRATEGIES—
The Art of Rhetoric

Rhetoric is the art (some might say the science) of putting words, phrases, sentences, and paragraphs together strategically and purposefully in order to communicate with one's audience.

In any rhetorical situation, we have an intended receiver in mind; for instance, the act of writing something down presupposes that the document we create is destined to be read—even if, as with a personal diary, that reader is the self. Usually, though—and especially in academic and professional situations—the readers and/or listeners are others: we refer to these intended receivers of our words as our *audience*.

We can define this audience in many ways, usually based on some aspect of human demographics: we can consider factors that are geographical, cultural, and even philosophical.

Can you think of some other ways in which we can define audience?

Could any of these factors influence what you write and how you write it?

- Age (e.g., high school students, senior citizens)
- Level of education (e.g., general public, postsecondary)
- Socioeconomic status (e.g., marginalized groups, privileged)

Note that unless the writer explicitly states the intended audience, our discussion of target audience must be speculative. Similarly, in our own writing, we do not have to make an overt statement about who our audience is—but we should have a sense of the intended reader of our document in order to effectively frame what we say and how we say it.

Our sense of audience will definitely shape our *tone* (our apparent attitude toward the subject) and our *diction* (our choice of words).

Connected to audience is the idea of purpose: why are we writing? A purpose of explanation is called *expository*; a purpose of argument is called *persuasive*. A *thesis* (main argument) reflects a persuasive aim; however, persuasion often makes use expository modes as well:

- Elements of *definition* and/or *description* give necessary information about the subject under discussion.

- *Narration* gives anecdotal material, telling a relevant story to develop the topic.

We also need to be aware of how we set up any given discussion. How do we arrange our ideas? Again, the answer is related to our underlying sense of purpose.

Patterns of arrangement have to do with the way in which we organize our discussion of any given topic. If we are discussing a series of events or steps in a *process*, a *chronological* pattern of arrangement would make the most sense; note that this pattern is the only one that merits the use of chronological transitions such as first, next, and so forth. A *spatial* pattern of arrangement would work effectively for a physical description of something. A *climactic* pattern of arrangement builds from least to most important.

We can consider both audience and purpose in two ways when thinking about an academic context. In one way, your audience is the postsecondary English expert reading your work, and your purpose is to convince that person that you are competent to communicate ideas at the university level. In another way, each question will have an inherent sense of audience and purpose. In any case, always ask yourself before you begin writing, "Who is my audience here? What is my purpose in this discussion?"

Consider a common scenario, in which you need to contact one of your professors to make a request of some kind. The choice of topic is up to you; consider these prompts as possibilities: you need to miss a class, you need clarification on an assignment, you need to reschedule an examination, and so forth.

Here's an example of what NOT to do:

From: foxychick@hotmail.com
Subject:
hey prof–
i wanna know what we done in class last time???? and also could u rise my mark on that last thing we did cuz i tried real hard & i need to higher my gpa !

Consider tone and diction, as well as persuasive impact (or lack thereof); are any of these requests likely to be granted? Are any expository elements missing?

Now try creating a positive model of a request e-mail to a professor. You will also have the opportunity to respond to a classmates' e-mail.

Discussion and Writing Opportunity: From Exposition to Persuasion—An E-mail to a Professor

_____

_____

_____

_____

_____

_____

_____

_____

_____

_____

_____

_____

_____

_____

_____

_____

_____

_____

_____

_____

_____

_____

_____

_____

_____

_____

_____

_____

_____

Next, switch with a classmate, and get that person to respond to the e-mail accordingly:

_____

_____

_____

_____

_____

_____

_____

_____

_____

_____

_____

_____

_____

_____

_____

_____

_____

_____

_____

_____

_____

_____

_____

_____

_____

_____

_____

Paragraphing

Specific requirements may differ as we write in various contexts (e.g., a brochure for publication, a formal report at work, an article for a newspaper or newsletter, an essay in an academic course), but all paragraphs share the quality of helping the reader to isolate distinct units of meaning within and among groups of sentences.

What makes a paragraph work well? First, we should distinguish between types of paragraphs based on purpose. Sometimes, a paragraph needs to stand on its own as a unique piece of writing. This type of paragraph is a stand-alone paragraph.

A stand-alone paragraph usually features a topic sentence (see in the following), including a brief hook to interest the reader, as well as effectively chosen and well-connected ideas on the topic. The final sentence often includes a sense of closure. In a standard essay, we have an introduction, body paragraphs, and a conclusion.

Paragraph Format

Academic assignments usually follow a standard protocol that includes double-spacing (no extra space between paragraphs) and indentation of the first word (typically five spaces). The length of a standard paragraph in an academic paper, although we see some variations, may be one-third to two-thirds of a page long, perhaps around one hundred words, and five to ten sentences (depending on sentence length and complexity).

Topic Sentences

In an introduction paragraph, we usually have a hook (such as an anecdote or interesting background information) to engage the reader's attention. Then, we lead into the main point or argument of the essay, the thesis.

This thesis statement is often the final sentence of the introduction, and it serves the dual purpose of answering the topic question at hand, by making a defensible persuasive statement, as well as forecasting, by means of keywords, the topics of the subsequent body paragraphs.

Each body paragraph will typically have a topic sentence, although such a topic sentence is not necessarily the first (nor the last) sentence in the paragraph; it may be embedded, or even simply implied. The body paragraphs should furnish specific proof of the paper's thesis, by means of particular illustrative examples.

The conclusion paragraph may begin with a reaffirmation (in reworded form) of the thesis; however, a good conclusion will do more than simply repeat and/or summarize previous points. Try to move beyond the limitations of the specific topic to a broader or more general context—the big picture, if you will—and, although you are giving a sense of closure, avoid implying that you have said all one could possibly say about the topic.

Consider the broader issues of humanity/the future/life, and so forth. Aim (though this goal is difficult to achieve) to be somewhat profound. Without introducing new examples, leave the reader with something to think about.

Paragraph Development

Note that in a multiparagraph composition for many academic and professional contexts, we aim for a balanced sense of development; thus, all paragraphs are approximately the same length (i.e., several sentences).

The standard minimum number of paragraphs for an essay is at least four or five, including introduction and conclusion. (As you have no doubt observed, journalism [including online modes] varies widely from this model, with very short paragraphs as the norm). Within each paragraph, sentence variety will create a visually and intellectually appealing document.

Unity and Coherence

Regardless of context, a good paragraph is both unified (all ideas clearly on topic) and coherent (smoothly flowing from one point to the next). Coherence means that the reader should never be left with a sense of confusion about how you got from point A to point B in your thinking as a writer; the connection between ideas may be evident to you (implicit, or understood), but it needs to be clear for the audience as well (explicit, or stated overtly).

You may achieve this with a transition of addition ("moreover," "in addition," etc.), contrast ("however," "nonetheless," etc.), or example ("for instance," etc.). Sometimes, you may need an entire sentence to transition from one idea to the next. A useful strategy is to use a keyword from the previous sentence (e.g., end of the previous paragraph) in the next sentence (e.g., beginning of the next paragraph).

Transitions

Within and between paragraphs, we should see clear transitions connecting the ideas. Avoid transitions of chronology (firstly, etc.) where the only inherent order is the one imposed by you as the writer; instead, consider logical links between concepts.

Consider this example from a student paper: it began, "On the one hand"; the next paragraph started, "On the other hand"; and the following paragraphs were as follows: "On the third hand," "On the fourth hand," and "On the fifth hand." The student failed to consider that the transition (contrast) metaphor of hands is taken from human anatomy.

Drafting the Essay

The writing process can be intimidating unless we break it down into stages rather than simply focusing on the finished project. By drafting, or prewriting, before we submit the final copy of the document, we can ensure a higher level of writing and a reduced level of stress.

Prewriting is what we do before we start drafting a piece of writing. It's like the warm-up you do before you go for a distance run: not part of the exercise, but something that makes it easier and better if you do it first! Now, some people just like to start running with no stretching beforehand, just as some people like to start writing without this type of preparation. However, take this coach's advice: give it a try and see if it improves your technique!

Often, we feel a certain escalation of energy and perhaps tension as a deadline approaches. To some extent, this phenomenon is inescapable, and we may naturally speed up near the end of a task. What we may wish to consider, though, is a different mode whereby we have a sustained level of positive energy throughout the process, without the hampering effects of increased tension at the end.

Another key component is the ability to have time at the conclusion of the writing process to read over, and edit (at a macro- and microlevel), what we've written. If you are handing in something you just finished writing, you are probably doing yourself (and your readers) something of a disservice. You owe it to yourself (and to them) to review your writing at least briefly.

Thus, what we need to do is not speed up at the end, but actually slow down. But how to do it? One strategy designed to achieve this positive result endorsed by many teachers and students of writing is the creation and implementation of a false deadline.

In an in-class writing situation, you need to set your mental alarm clock so you stop writing whatever you feel is adequate time to review what you've written. You have to take this lie seriously, though: don't be thinking, "well, I really do have that extra time . . ." Pretend you don't! Adjust the lie as needed in other situations.

Next time you face a deadline, as you reach the end point, you will be calmly reading over what you've written, perhaps making a few changes, slowing down and thinking about it, not ramping it up but ramping it down. Try it! The following are some specific prewriting strategies that you may find useful in the drafting process.

Overcoming Mental Blocks: Freewriting, Mind Mapping, Brainstorming, and Questioning

The primary type of prewriting is freewriting. As promoted by American writing teacher Peter Elbow, this exercise helps you to get past a mental block. If you've ever sat there trying to start an assignment, thinking, "I have no idea what to write," or "Isn't it interesting how that crack in the ceiling somewhat resembles a giant rabbit?" or "I'm so hungry—why didn't I eat that banana for breakfast this morning?" . . . then this strategy could be for you!

With freewriting, you just start writing continuously whatever comes into your head, whether it's on topic or not: in doing so, you break down the barrier between brain and pen, and thus you may be able to go on in a more focused and productive manner. Your writing is in sentence/paragraph form, like a diary or journal in some respects.

Another valuable strategy is brainstorming. This may be the one promoted most frequently by many teachers (not much of an endorsement, really, unless you want to end up as an English teacher). With this exercise, you record only ideas that are on topic, but you don't need to worry about putting them into sentence form (as this type of prewriting is done in point form), and you don't need to worry about how they relate to each other (as you record them in random order).

Later, you can look back at what you have come up with, see which ideas seem to have the most potential, and start writing a draft accordingly.

A variation on the theme earlier is called clustering, branching, or mind mapping (and perhaps you have learned it by yet another name). This one is tremendously popular; it has appeared on countless student compositions over the years. It looks like a tree or a series of bubbles or squares connected by lines, and it enables you to very clearly see the connections between ideas, which ideas derive directly from others, and so forth.

For this exercise, you would use keywords or phrases—it would be too cumbersome to do it with larger semantic units. Once you've completed your diagram, the challenge is to convert it into the basis of a coherent essay!

Finally, perhaps the most challenging prewriting exercise is called questioning. Try taking the W5 reporter's questions (who/what/when/where/why) and create some thought-provoking questions.

You do not always need to answer these questions—sometimes just asking them is enough to make you and your reader think productively about the topic; a rhetorical question can be tremendously effective in an essay. Just remember, these questions have to be complex enough to take you down an interesting path . . .

So, here is prewriting in a nutshell (see in the following)!

You can and should try any and all that work for you.

Freewriting

  — Helps overcome a mental block

  — Continuous prose

  — Stream of consciousness

  — Individual activity

Brainstorming

  — Helps generate ideas

  — Point form notes

  — Random order

  — Individual or partner or group activity

Clustering/Branching/Mind Mapping

  — Helps discover related ideas

  — Diagram

  — Shows connections between ideas

  — Individual activity

Questioning

  — Helps explore provocative aspects of the topic

  — "W5" reporter's questions

  — Perhaps questions > answers

  — Individual or partner or group activity

"As to my own part, having turned my thoughts for many years, upon this important subject, and maturely weighed the several schemes of our projectors, I have always found them grossly mistaken in their computation."

—*Jonathan Swift, "A Modest Proposal"*

FREEWRITING PRACTICE

Write continuously for ten minutes; for a random prompt, open a dictionary and pick a word to get you started.

BRAINSTORMING PRACTICE

Think of a task you need to accomplish in school, at your job, or in your personal life. With a partner, jot down in point form all the ideas you can think of that are relevant to this task. Subsequently, take a highlighter and indicate which are the best ideas; use different highlighters if you wish to divide the ideas into categories. If the ideas relate to a sequential (chronological) process, put numbers beside them. Now do the same with your partner for your partner's task.

MIND-MAPPING PRACTICE

Choose a topic that you are interested in from current events, from one of our readings, or from any other context. Put that topic in the box in the center of the page, then create a branching diagram with other boxes (or other shapes) to explore related ideas.

QUESTIONING PRACTICE

Think of an issue that is a hot topic (interesting/controversial). What thought-provoking questions arise from thinking about it? Remember, you do not need to know the answers!

TOPIC:

QUESTIONS:

Outlining

One of the very tangible skills we can import into our repertoire is that of structuring a discussion clearly, with a good sense of where we are going with it—before we actually start writing.

A formal outline, while it may seem on the surface to be potentially constraining or limiting due to its somewhat rigid structure, actually can be tremendously liberating: with the key ideas set in place, we now have the freedom to think about what words we will choose, and how we can best create effective sentences and paragraphs to convey our thoughts with concision and grace.

Creating a sentence outline allows us to record a thesis and main points in preparation for a well-structured essay. Many students have some experience of making a rough outline, but this is a more focused and directed attempt, as we practice preparing a formal outline in sentence form.

It all starts with a great title, which shows the choice of topic. Then the thesis, in sentence form, offers a direct argument in response to the topic question and foregrounds, by means of keywords, the points to come in the subsequent body paragraphs.

Each body paragraph idea comes after a Roman numeral (I., II., etc.), perhaps with even further details (A., B., etc.), and possibly even more (1., 2.; a., b.; i., ii . . .). Each category requires at least two parts—and everything is in complete sentence form. No need for an introduction or conclusion—you can write those later as part of the essay itself.

Do yourself the favor of preparing some well-structured planning and outlining. Submitting the outline itself is usually not necessary—and, in fact, some people can even do it in their heads . . . In any case, if this strategy works effectively for you, an outline can be a useful tool!

Here is a sample outline rubric, followed by a sample outline for a "literary" topic:

- Title specs as per Modern Language Association (MLA) guidelines
- Thesis as one sentence
- Each point and subpoint as one sentence each
- Roman numerals for main points representing body paragraphs
- Capital letters for subpoints (then numbers, then small letters, then small Roman numerals)
- At least two items per category (no A without B, no 1 without 2, etc.)
- Consistent double-spacing
- Consistent font
- Consistent margins
- Appropriate grammar and formal academic writing style

Sample Outline

John Jacob Jingleheimer Schmidt

Prof D Blenkhorn

ENGL 2316 S10

21 Nov 2019

Formal Outline

Beowulf's Legacy in Popular Culture

Thesis: *Beowulf* prefigures the heroic characterization, supernatural thematic elements, and rugged setting of the modern film classics *The Lion King*, *Pirates of the Caribbean*, and *Madagascar*, respectively.

I.   As a hero, Beowulf goes through different stages of maturity, as does Simba.

    A.   Beowulf starts out in his prime and ends up an old man.

    B.   Simba grows from a cub to a mature leader.

II.   Supernatural elements in *Beowulf* and *Pirates* indicate a spiritual theme.

III.   A rugged setting adds to the adventure of both *Beowulf* and *Madagascar*.

Expository and Persuasive Writing

If we are reading a textbook, an article, a novel, a report, and so forth, we can write a summary of it and perhaps even explain it to someone else. This is expository writing. However, in a university course, you will need to go beyond that basic understanding in order to show that you have been thinking analytically about the topic and blending new information with other knowledge to produce a fresh perspective and to convince others of its viability. We need to start with what we know—and then we need to take it to the next level through a process of *critical thinking*.

Even if you're not sure exactly what critical thinking is, you can likely imagine the opposite of critical thinking. If we simply accept what we hear, see, or read at face value, without questioning, we are not thinking critically about it. On the other hand, if we probe beneath the surface—if we consider the consequences and implications of what we encounter—we are on the critical path to enlightenment.

Let's consider our understanding of the following components of thinking critically; write down a definition and/or example of each of these:

— objectivity _____

— knowledge _____

— wisdom _____

— understanding _____

— experience _____

— questioning _____

— logic _____

— reasoning _____

— analysis _____

— synthesis _____

How to Convince an Oppositional Audience

Logos (logic), ethos (ethics), and pathos (sympathy/empathy) are all ways of persuading one's audience, as originally described by Aristotle of the ancient Greeks.

We may also consider the value of *concession and refutation*. In any argument, we may see a concession to the opposing side; an acknowledgment of the validity of the opposing point of view. Nonetheless, to make our argument strong, we need to issue a clear confirmation of our own side, which necessarily involves refutation against our antagonists.

Crafting a Viable Thesis Statement

The word thesis comes from hypothesis, a key element in the standard model of enquiry for university-level research. The hypothesis requires proof. In other words, in university-level writing, we will not simply be presenting facts.

We will be proving a theory: perhaps the theory itself will be original, perhaps we will be proving it using a new method or with different evidence; perhaps we will be synthesizing the data in a unique way.

An introduction to a formal essay usually begins with a hook of some kind to capture the reader's attention. Standard strategies include background material, an interesting fact or thought, perhaps an anecdote.

The introductory paragraph does not begin directly with the thesis; the thesis goes at the end of the introduction. The writer's task is to take two or three sentences to get from the hook to the thesis. The introduction is the same length as other paragraphs in the document, approximately one-third to two-thirds of a page.

The thesis is a direct answer to the topic question. It needs to make an argument (which must be defensible and controversial; it should not be an argument that everyone would already agree with).

The thesis is one sentence at the end of the introduction paragraph. It should mention keywords relating to the subtopics to be developed in the subsequent body paragraphs. It must be a statement about the topic, not about the essay itself or about what the writer will do.

Understanding Logic: Inductive and Deductive Reasoning, Syllogisms, Fallacies

One fundamental process of logic is induction. We start with known examples, put them together, and figure out what we can conclude as a result. We are reasoning inward from specifics to a general conclusion in this model (note the Latin prefix in-):

X _____

Y _____

Z _____

Q _____

. . . from which we induce _____

The opposite approach is deduction. Here, we are reasoning outward from a thesis to specifics (note the Latin prefix de-):

Based on the idea that _____ we can deduce that

A _____

B _____

C _____

D _____

Putting facts and ideas from various sources in different words (let alone quoting them directly) will not be sufficient to show that we have thought critically about the topic. It can be a daunting task! So where do we begin? With *syllogisms*: if you've studied set theory, this should all sound somewhat familiar.

We start with what we know:

This knowledge becomes our major premise . . .

For example, all x are A.

We follow with a minor premise . . .

For example, sample belongs to x.

And hence the conclusion . . .

For example, sample belongs to A.

We have the ancient Greeks to thank for this syllogistic structure. They thought the philosopher Socrates was so great that some people questioned whether he might be immortal like the gods. Was he immortal? Logic provided the answer. The classic example was as follows: All men are mortal. Socrates is a man. Therefore, Socrates is mortal.

If a syllogism works properly and is based on an accurate major premise, it is valid.

If it leads to a known fact, it is true. But it can be true without being valid.

You can see how the syllogism could go wrong if the major premise is wrong . . .

All birds lay eggs. Penguins are birds. Penguins lay eggs. Good! True and valid.

All birds can fly. A robin is a bird. A robin can fly. Oops! True but not valid.

All birds can fly. A penguin is a bird. Whoops! What's the conclusion? Is it true?

When we read or listen to someone's ideas, we can ask ourselves if the argument in question has both truth and validity.

It goes without saying (or should) that an opinion cannot be the basis of a logical argument.

Of course, logic (or LOGOS, as the ancient Greeks called it) is not the only means of persuasion. Other powerful strategies are PATHOS (emotion) and ETHOS (ethics)—but these latter two strategies have a component of subjectivity, whereas logic has a mathematical objectivity that leads to certainty in a way the other persuasive strategies cannot.

Why does it all matter? As George Orwell argued, only by having citizens who think for themselves can we hope for a better society . . . think about it!

Fallacies: When Logic Goes Wrong

Find examples in contemporary media of the following:

non sequitur/It does not follow.

One point does not logically lead to the next.

_____

post hoc ergo propter hoc/After this therefore because of this.

Just because something precedes something else does not mean it caused it.

_____

ad populum/To the people.

Just because many people think something does not mean it is right.

_____

ad hominem/To the man.

Do not confuse personality with the real issues in the argument.

_____

Red herring

Do not be led astray by an irrelevant issue, interesting though it may be.

_____

Begging the question

Do not make assumptions.

_____

Equivocation

Do not mix up the meanings when a word has more than one meaning.

_____

Developmental Strategies: Cause and Effect, Process, Classification and Division, Comparison and Contrast

Cause and effect is a mode of essay development whereby the focus is on the reasons for something and/or its results. In putting together such an argument, we need to be particularly aware of the analogy of false cause, or *post hoc ergo propter hoc*.

Just because something precedes something else does not indicate a causal relationship. Nor should we come to a hasty generalization, that is, making a conclusion based on lack of adequate evidence.

Classification refers to understanding a concept in terms of types; division refers to the idea of dividing something into parts. Both of these strategies or modes of development are common in essays in which we are trying to take a creative and original approach to a topic. The challenge is to do so in a way that makes our readers reconsider the subject from the perspective of critical thinking.

Comparison and contrast as a development mode focuses on similarities and differences, respectively—although sometimes when we are asked to write a comparative essay, the assumption is that we will look at both what is similar and what is different. We need to be wary of the faulty analogy, a fallacy in which the juxtaposition/comparison makes little sense.

Here is a quick overview of these modes:

- A *cause and effect* mode of development explores the reasons behind something (cause) and/or the results (effect).

- *Classification* as a mode of development serves to place something within a broader category or type; *division* takes a larger concept and subcategorizes it into smaller units.

- *Comparison* seeks to show the analogies or similarities between two or more phenomena, whereas *contrast* highlights the differences.

Using any of the earlier, prepare a brief (five-minute) presentation on a topic of your choice; choose a subject of which you have personal knowledge, rather than preparing a research-based speech.

Presentations

Use this PEER FEEDBACK FORM to offer feedback to a partner:

Preparation/planning?

_____

_____

_____

Interesting focus on topic?

_____

_____

_____

Posture/voice/eye contact?

_____

_____

_____

Audience engagement?

_____

_____

_____

Structure (intro/development/conclusion)?

_____

_____

_____

General comments/overall impression?

_____

_____

_____

"I am a writer. And by that definition, I am someone who has always loved language. I am fascinated by language in daily life. I spend a great deal of my time thinking about the power of language — the way it can evoke an emotion, a visual image, a complex idea, or a simple truth."

—*Amy Tan, "Mother Tongue"*

Review Exercise: Putting Together a Logical Argument

WORKSHEET A

IDENTIFY AND DESCRIBE THREE SOCIAL ISSUES ABOUT WHICH WE MAY THINK CRITICALLY; FOR THIS FIRST STAGE, JUST DEFINE EACH ISSUE RATHER THAN ARGUING ABOUT IT OR PRESENTING OPINIONS . . .

1.

_____

_____

_____

_____

_____

_____

2.

_____

_____

_____

_____

_____

_____

_____

3.

_____

_____

_____

_____

_____

_____

_____

WORKSHEET B

CHOOSE ONE ISSUE THAT HAS CLEARLY OPPOSING ARGUMENTS ON BOTH SIDES OF A PUBLIC DEBATE; COME UP WITH SEVERAL POINTS ON EACH SIDE OF THE DEBATE . . .

PRO:

_____

_____

_____

_____

_____

_____

_____

_____

_____

_____

_____

CON:

_____

_____

_____

_____

_____

_____

_____

_____

_____

_____

_____

WORKSHEET C

IDENTIFY WHICH PERSUASIVE APPEALS MAY APPLY TO THE ARGUMENT, INDICATING IN BRACKETS WHETHER EACH APPEAL APPLIES TO THE PRO OR CON SIDE OF THE DEBATE:

ETHOS:

_____

_____

_____

_____

_____

_____

_____

_____

PATHOS:

_____

_____

_____

_____

_____

_____

_____

LOGOS:

_____

_____

_____

_____

_____

_____

_____

WORKSHEET D

IDENTIFY ANY LOGICAL FALLACIES IN THE DEBATE, AGAIN INDICATING IN BRACKETS TO WHICH SIDE OF THE ARGUMENT YOU ATTRIBUTE THEM:

_____

_____

_____

_____

_____

_____

_____

_____

_____

_____

_____

_____

_____

_____

_____

_____

_____

_____

_____

_____

_____

_____

_____

_____

_____

_____

_____

WORKSHEET E

CREATE AN OUTLINE FOR PRESENTATION OF THE ISSUE OF YOUR CHOICE; YOUR PRESENTATION SHOULD CLEARLY REVEAL THAT YOU HAVE ENGAGED IN THE PROCESS OF CRITICAL THINKING

_____

_____

_____

_____

_____

_____

_____

_____

_____

_____

_____

_____

_____

_____

_____

_____

_____

_____

_____

_____

_____

_____

_____

_____

_____

SECTION 4

RHETORICAL ANALYSIS—
Reflections on Writing

Recalling that _rhetoric_ is speech or writing for a purpose, we can see that analyzing the rhetorical strategies of someone else's work, writing about writing, can help us become better writers, as well as leading us to an appreciation of the content and style of what we are analyzing. Our first impressions of what we read, hear, or see are individual and personal.

Objectivity at the initial stage of first contact isn't possible—and, arguably, not even desirable. We need to come to terms with our subjective response before we can take an objective and/or critical viewpoint, before we can effectively analyze.

Previous experience and inherent preferences shape our response to any stimulus, and recording that first response can be a source of satisfaction and enlightenment as we embark on the analytical process.

As a prelude to the analytical process, which includes the stages of reader-response, summary, critical reading, and essay writing, we can explore the exercise of doing a Reader's Journal, in which we write down our candid response to what we read.

This first assignment in the current chapter solicits your candid and sincere thoughts on some of our reading materials for this course; each entry needs to be a minimum of 150 words (choose two selected Readings from our text). Here is an overview of what instructors typically look for in a Reader's Journal:

- Connections to the student reader's own personal life

- A sense of inspiration

- Insights about life, society, human psychology, and so forth

- Awareness of the details of the literary craft: the form of each piece, the strategies, and devices employed by the author

- Willingness to admit the parts that are challenging to understand

- Taking a risk of making an interpretation that is beyond the superficial or obvious

- Talk about engaging in discussion of the work with other people such as friends or family

- Remembrance of having studied (or otherwise encountered) the work in the past

- Making connections between/among the works on the syllabus (and beyond to other works in other contexts)

- Anything else you deem interesting or relevant—which may include objective critique or analysis

Discussion and Writing Opportunity: From Personal Response to Objective Analysis

READER'S JOURNAL 1

TITLE	AUTHOR

READER'S JOURNAL 2

TITLE	AUTHOR

Comprehension

It goes without saying (if anything does), we cannot start analyzing something until we're sure we understand it first. The ability to summarize the main ideas of someone else's writing is a necessary first step. How can we be sure we've covered all the bases?

One tried-and-true remedy comes from the world of journalism, where reporters constantly face the pressure of looming deadlines. Unless they capture directly and efficiently the essentials of a news feature, they'll lose their job! The "W5" formula journalists developed (and indeed, "W5" became a famous news program) is useful for all of us as writers.

Try taking the W5 reporter's questions (who/what/when/where/why) and create some thought-provoking questions. You do not always need to answer these questions—sometimes just asking them is enough to make you and your reader think productively about the topic; a rhetorical question can be tremendously effective in an essay. Just remember, these questions have to be complex enough to take you down an interesting path. Try doing W5 questions for any two readings.

We can also think about some ways in which we can transfer our learning to real-world contexts. For instance, the insight that great writers are (more often than not) great readers may prompt us to do more—and better—reading. But how can we be sure we are retaining what we hope to get out of it? How can we hang on to what we read in such a way that it really does inform and inspire our own writing?

Writing a summary allows us to take someone else's great ideas and put them into our own words. A surefire way of checking that we've got the main points is asking the Reporter's Questions, so try the tried-and-true W5 approach (asking who, what, when, where, and why), then paraphrase away! By using your own words, you guarantee not only that you have identified key issues, but that you understand the content.

Leave the examples and illustrative material behind, and stick to the main ideas, bearing in mind how long (or short!) your summary is supposed to be. Create a coherent, concise, stand-alone new version of the original.

Economize, summarize—and then you'll be ready to analyze. Meanwhile, the next time you read something you want to keep as part of your repertoire, put together a quick summary for future reference. Maybe post it in your e-portfolio or blog if you have one. It's a minimal amount of time and effort for something that could last you a lifetime!

"It is not words only that are emblematic; it is things which are emblematic. Every natural fact is a symbol of some spiritual fact. Every appearance in nature corresponds to some state of the mind, and that state of the mind can only be described by presenting that natural appearance as its picture. An enraged man is a lion, a cunning man is a fox, a firm man is a rock, a learned man is a torch. A lamb is innocence; a snake is subtle spite; flowers express to us the delicate affections. Light and darkness are our familiar expression for knowledge and ignorance; and heat for love. Visible distance behind and before us, is respectively our image of memory and hope."

—*Ralph Waldo Emerson, "Language"*

PROTOCOLS FOR CRITIQUE AND ANALYSIS: COMPREHENSION EXERCISE

NAME OF AUTHOR	TITLE OF READING

WHO	
WHAT	
WHEN	
WHERE	
WHY	

NAME OF AUTHOR	TITLE OF READING

WHO	
WHAT	
WHEN	
WHERE	
WHY	

Summarizing

Now, let's work on turning one of these into a summary document. Imagine that you want to provide a condensed version of the original piece of writing itself. Focus on main ideas rather than specific examples, instances, or illustrative points. Think about answering the W5 questions in a more general way: Mr. X, Ms. Y, and Dr. Z may be named in the original document; the more general answer to the "Who?" question would be to identify their role (research scientists). Think the same way about specific locations, and so forth.

Sometimes you may need to figure out the general concept behind a specific detail. Writer Amy Tan talks about how although her mother reads *Forbes* magazine and *Wall Street Week*, people don't take her seriously because her English is limited: can you find the principle behind this example, without mentioning the author, her mother, or the specific publications?

Do not use up your word count with unnecessary phrasing about the author and article: just state the points of the document directly. Try to reflect the author's argument or thesis as accurately as you can. The challenge in writing about other people's writing is to maintain appropriate verb tenses throughout the discussion. Present tense is necessary to talk about what the author says in the article, and is a requirement for facts, habits, truth, and so forth. Past tense is for history and events that took place in the past, and so forth. The present perfect tense is often useful as well.

As always in academic writing, maintain a level of formality and professionalism appropriate to the context (e.g., avoid contractions). Note: This guideline holds true regardless of the language in the document you are summarizing, so occasionally you may find that your language is more formal than that of the original document. For instance, the document may use casual language ("kids, moms, and dads"), but you would substitute more formal diction ("children and parents").

Finally, check and double check for spelling mistakes, missing words, and so forth. Note that commas and periods go inside quotation marks (where you have no parenthetical reference), according to Modern Language Association (MLA) protocols: "as such," and "so on."

Let's consider a few examples of stand-alone summaries; you can find the original articles in Section 7 to provide context, but these condensed versions should make sense on their own. Once you have read through these sample summaries, choose one of the articles from the W5 exercise and create your own summary paragraph of 100–150 words.

SAMPLE SUMMARY # 1

Multiple Englishes: A Summary of Amy Tan's "Mother Tongue"

We often think of English as a single language, but actually people learn diverse versions of English as their mother tongue. Language development is the product of the influence of both peers and family. Native English speakers may see these variations as inferior, particularly among more insular families such as those of immigrants, and those who speak English as an additional language may be the victims of discrimination accordingly. Perceptions of English, and indeed the study of English, can be quite subjective. Judgment calls, as opposed to hard answers, can vary greatly. Children from some immigrant families may receive advice to steer away from the literary arts by teachers and mentors who believe that their language skills are deficient. Yet language proficiency tests only assess the technical, not accounting for any number of the nuances that an author may want to convey; people with technically imperfect English should receive encouragement rather than facing barriers. They may develop a technical understanding of the language, but still have a valid reason to write in their mother tongue.

Work Cited

Tan, Amy. "Mother Tongue." *Dreams and Inward Journeys: A Rhetoric and Reader for Writers*, edited by Marjorie Ford and Jon Ford, Pearson, 7th ed., 2010, pp. 34–44.

SAMPLE SUMMARY # 2

Making It Work: A Summary of Orwell's "Politics and the English Language"

Although most people think the English language is declining, they tend to also think we cannot reverse the process because it is part of a general social decline. In fact, we can and should try to improve our use of language as a means to bringing about positive social change. Some writers and politicians—including well-known, respected figures—are too lazy to pay careful attention to the way they use English, while others are trying too hard to sound impressive without considering whether people can actually understand what they are saying. Many bad habits of English usage require consideration in improving our ability to communicate clearly and thus in improving our society.

Work Cited

Orwell, George. "Politics and the English Language." *Horizon*, vol. 13, no. 76, 1946, pp. 252–65.

SAMPLE SUMMARY # 3

De-Cluttering: A Summary of William Zinsser's "Simplicity"

As a close look at American writing shows, authors need to communicate in a clearer and more straightforward manner. In business, as elsewhere in society, those who compose various documents are trying so hard to sound important that they make everything they write unnecessarily complicated—so much so that readers and listeners have become suspicious of plain language. The more educated or high-ranking people are, the more elevated—and unclear—their language becomes. They would be better off eliminating unnecessary or redundant words and using simple phrasing that others can easily understand. Great writers are able to achieve this lack of clutter because their thinking itself is clear and uncluttered. After all, readers have many demands upon their limited attention span, and any misuse of language by careless writers only adds to the confusion and lack of engagement. Writing well, to produce material that makes for easy and enjoyable reading, is hard work.

Work Cited

Zinsser, William. "Simplicity." *On Writing Well*, Harper & Row, 1978, pp. 6–11.

SUMMARY EXERCISE

Now, try and write your own, one-paragraph, stand-alone summaries of 100–150 words. Choose any two of the readings from our text. Your title is the first impression you make on your reader—so make it a good one! At a bare minimum, the title of a summary will usually include the word Summary (note that you are writing a summary, not the [i.e., the only] summary) and the title (in double quotes) of the document you are summarizing. A stronger title could also include the name of the author and some phrasing indicating the focus of the piece. Note capitalization protocols: capitalize the first letter of each word other than articles, prepositions, and conjunctions (except the first word of the title or first word after a colon). Do not underline or italicize your title.

Here is a review chart of the criteria for our stand-alone summary assignment:

DO	DO NOT
→ Include the main ideas from the original passage	✗ Include details (including most names, numbers, etc.)
→ Use your own words	✗ Borrow phrasing from the original
→ Offer a condensed paraphrase	✗ Use quotes
→ Put the name of the author and article in the title of your summary	✗ Mention the author or the article in the summary itself
→ Represent the argument of the article directly and without judgment	✗ Include your own personal views on the topic
→ Put forward only the ideas in the document itself	✗ Refer to any secondary sources
→ Use an objective viewpoint	✗ Use first-person subjective "I" anywhere in the summary
→ Use a formal, academic writing style	✗ Use casual, informal, or slang diction (regardless of the style of the original)
→ Observe the assignment length guidelines of one coherent paragraph, 100–150 words	✗ Deviate from the requirements in terms of coherence or length

"Nothing is easier than to admit in words
the truth of the universal struggle for life, or
more difficult—at least I have found it so—than
constantly to bear this conclusion in mind."

—*Charles Darwin, The Origin of Species*

SUMMARY A

AUTHOR	ARTICLE

TITLE	

SUMMARY B

AUTHOR	ARTICLE

TITLE	

Critical Reading

Even if you have been an avid reader all your life, you need to start being a critical reader when you are taking university-level courses. What is critical reading? Reading critically involves being aware of and thinking about the ideas presented and the way they are expressed. The thing about reading critically is that once you've started doing it, you can't go back to reading uncritically.

You may actually lose the ability to read something without being sensitive to the way in which it articulates its concepts. What does this mean in practical terms? Well, on a lighter note (perhaps) it means that you may begin to notice every grammatical, typographical, logistical, and stylistic issue arising in everything you read, even when you're reading for pleasure (e.g., a mystery novel) or to get information (e.g., from the newspaper, or even from a sign in a grocery store or at a bus stop). What's wrong with telling people that "buses only pick up passengers at designated stops"? (Think about it—hint: the modifier "only" is misplaced).

How do you get started? It works a bit differently for everyone, but some useful tips are as follows: read everything more than once (the first time just for interest, enjoyment, and to get the general idea; then subsequently to pick up on the nuances and details); annotate (write things in the margin or on a separate sheet of paper or cue card—questions, observations, connections to other authors, and ideas you're familiar with).

Evaluate the ideas and the words the author has chosen to convey them in terms of their logic, their viability, their appeal; don't just accept it all at face value; do your best to understand it at a deep level, but don't assume that you're always the one at fault if it doesn't make sense.

What's the deal about all this, anyway? George Orwell, in "Politics and the English Language" (see Section 7) insists that such matters are not just the concern of English professors: he tells us that reading and writing and thinking constitutes a package. Or maybe a better metaphor would be to say that they are all part of a cycle. When one of these aspects gets sloppy or inaccurate, the others do, too, and eventually society degenerates into a hopeless mess. Orwell is actually an optimist, though. You may be familiar with his social critique and satire (*Animal Farm, 1984*)—the purpose of this writing is social correction, after all. If we start thinking about and working on what's wrong with society (and surely this begins with how we think and express our thoughts), we can change the world.

Orwell was writing in the middle of the previous century. How far have we come since then? Someone who has tried (and arguably succeeded in his own way) to achieve social change is author and filmmaker Michael Moore. Moore is a fan of Orwell and has quoted him publicly. Moore urges us to be particularly critical of what people in positions of authority (especially government) tell us, and how they consciously attempt to shape the way we see ourselves and the world around us. (If you are not yet familiar with Moore's films, try *Fahrenheit 9/11* or *Bowling for Columbine.*)

The question of how we think about ourselves and how society "reads" us—and how we "read" others—comes up in Ralph Waldo Emerson's discussion of "Language" (see Section 7). If we take the notion of reading critically to a level beyond what is simply verbal, we can start to consider "reading" in this expanded way, especially in terms of working toward a sense of what "critical reading" entails, and it's not a bad way to think about this course as a whole.

Social perception begins with the self. That's one of the themes of John Locke's writing, as he develops his "Essay Concerning Human Understanding." Locke encourages us to question the validity of some of the ideas we come across: as we read Locke's argument, we can consider it in light of persuasion and how to understand and evaluate logic.

Needless to say (or maybe not so needless), our perceptions of self and others are affected not only by individuals, but by authority, by government and by institutions. If you've given some thought to issues like this, you'll enjoy John Stuart Mill's treatise 'On Liberty' (see Section 7). Mill urges us to reevaluate and question some of our assumptions about the way the world works. How do we "read" the forces driving society today? We need to think behind social issues to the people themselves, the individuals who have rights and responsibilities. What and where is the spirit of humanity? Mill offers us a profound answer.

By the same token, Charles Darwin's discussion of "The Origin of Species" (see Section 7) leads to the exploration of the issue of thinking critically about science (e.g., evolution) and religion (e.g., creationism) and the arguments that arise from their practitioners. One of the challenges of critical reading is to be prepared to put aside our own preconceived notions, whatever they may be. Think laterally, not just literally! As Darwin innately seems to recognize, the focus of persuasion is to convince through presentation of logical paradigms.

Yet it's far from a new idea to examine society critically in this way—and even to poke fun at it in a controversial manner. Centuries ago and a continent away, Jonathan Swift was satirizing society centuries before our other social commentators were a glimmer in their parents' eyes. Whether you think of Swift as the Stephen Colbert of eighteenth-century Ireland or as the patron saint of satire, you can't help but admire his twisted sense of irony. The bottom line is that if you don't read Swift critically, you simply won't get it (and many didn't and still don't!) Again, the point is to think laterally, not literally.

Many people believe that the true masters of transcending the literal are storytellers. Fables by Aesop lead us to a new understanding of some fundamental (and sometimes harsh) truths about human existence.

In the next writing exercise, consider your own reading life, and feel free to refer to whichever authors have inspired you. Think about how you have developed your critical reading skills. You might also want to include other types of influences such as films or mentors.

Protocols for Critique and Analysis

Rhetorical analysis offers commentary on the author's use of writing strategies. Let's review the rhetorical strategies we looked at as the basis of argument and persuasion.

Ethos is ethics: what is right and wrong. We can think of ethos in terms of the way a writer presents himself or herself; we can also consider the ways in which a writer appeals to the ethical sense of the people for whom he or she is writing, that is, the audience. A powerful way of connecting to one's readership is to create a shared sense of ethos. Pathos is the Greek word from which we derive the English words sympathy and empathy; pathos has to do with the emotional component of rhetoric. If we sympathize, we understand, but at a distance; if we empathize, we feel the same way based on shared experience. Again, pathos can be a powerful persuasive tool. Logos is logic, powerful and irrefutable, with an almost mathematical certainty. Our moral sense of right and wrong is irrelevant, as are our emotions. Logic is the foundation of argument (although ethos and pathos often are part of persuasion) but it is vulnerable to fallacies (errors in reasoning) by those who do not use it wisely.

A rhetorical analysis, for our purposes in this course, is an essay about an article, telling what the article is about (in the intro) and then analyzing how the author uses ethos (ethics), pathos (sympathy/empathy), and logos (logic) in each of the body paragraphs, using at least one quotation per body paragraph. The thesis (at the end of the intro and beginning of the conclusion) is simply that the author uses ethos, pathos, and logos to convey the argument. The conclusion contextualizes the issue within a broader framework (society/humanity/history, etc.).

Aristotle of the ancient Greeks identified three modes of persuasion. Ethos can operate at (at least) two levels. The author may be showing us how ethical he/she is, or he/she may appeal to our sense of ethics regarding the issue(s) under discussion. For instance, if the author mentions that he is a faculty member at a school of medicine at a well-known institution, we are likely to attribute to him a high level of credibility in his field; we may also assume (rightly or wrongly), that doctors are responsible, intelligent pillars of the community. By the same token, an argument about environmental issues might appeal to our sense of ethos in assuming (again, rightly or wrongly) that we agree that all species are equally important as a value held by most if not all readers.

As an argumentative appeal, ethos breaks down when the assumptions are questionable: some medical researchers have been known to falsify their results for personal reasons (as in the case which led to the erroneous connection between vaccination and autism); adherents to a religion which preaches that human beings have a God-given dominion over everything on earth will judge an argument according to that particular value system, which may differ from that of the writer.

Pathos again can operate in two main ways. Sympathy allows us to feel for someone or something, even if we have no directly comparable experience; empathy is based on a shared sense of experience in which a direct connection is present. Canadian-born citizens can certainly sympathize with a Syrian refugee, but to say that they empathize with an immigrant or displaced person of any kind would be at best naive and at worst hypocritical. Pathos fails if the writer does not engage the reader's emotions, as is likely to happen when a student e-mails a professor to say, for the fifth time in the semester, that an assignment is incomplete because a beloved pet gerbil has died.

Logos is logic. If something simply makes sense with almost a mathematical certainty, it is logical. A syllogism takes a major premise, then a minor premise, then comes to a conclusion: All birds have wings; penguins are birds; therefore, penguins have wings. Not surprisingly, this type of appeal is the most irrefutable of the three. Inductive logic reasons inward to a general conclusion from a series of proofs; deductive reasoning begins with central assumption and reasons outward. As we have a thesis in mind when we write a persuasive essay, we tend to use the latter technique. Logic breaks down when it contains an error in reasoning, or fallacy, such as a hasty generalization (not enough evidence) or non sequitur (one point does not lead to the next).

Thus we can discuss any rhetorical situation (an article, a speech, etc.) in light of the ways in which it makes use of Aristotle's three appeals. Needless to say, we should also be aware of these in our own writing and speaking—if we want to effectively persuade our audience of what we are saying! Now, let's try putting together a Rhetorical Analysis essay. Choose an article from among our readings: make sure it is one in which you can identify the thesis, and comment on the author's use of ethos, pathos, and logos.

Sample Rhetorical Analysis Essay

Amy Tan and the Rhetoric of Family: An Analysis of "Mother Tongue"

What are the linguistic implications of growing up as the child of immigrant parents? A well-known American novelist urges us to consider this issue in an article she originally published in *The Threepenny Review* in 1990. In "Mother Tongue," Amy Tan argues that writers should be wary of pretentiousness in communicating their ideas. She insists that the use of complex language patterns is contrary to the true purpose of writing, interfering with meaning, and hampering the spirit of communication between author and reader. Tan uses the persuasive strategies of ethos, logos, and pathos to convey this argument to her audience of readers of contemporary popular fiction.

Among the ethical issues surrounding the use of language is the mistaken idea that we will sound more credible if we use more sophisticated words and complicated phrases. Tan begins by establishing her credibility as simply "a writer," as opposed to being an academic expert, and she makes the point that we will lose the comprehension and attention of our audience if we are merely trying to impress them. True credibility comes from sincere, genuine, and straightforward use of language, as Tan claims she suddenly realized during a public speech when she became aware of her own mother as one of her listeners. Tan goes on to narrate her personal experience of seeing how businesspeople and medical practitioners habitually display a lack of professional ethos as they treat her mother in a condescending manner, mistaking Mrs. Tan's simplicity for intellectual limitation.

Beyond the ethical arguments she puts forward in favor of simplifying and improving communication, Tan uses logos in providing evidence, such as the example of statistical proof that Asian students are more likely to pursue math, science, or business (as in her case, she was encouraged to "hone [her] talents toward account management"). She specifically references test performance as a supposedly logical criterion for determining students' aptitudes and abilities, while showing, ultimately, the limitations of taking what seem to be a logical approach to developing an effective learning and communication style. As much as Tan relies on facts and evidence to logically substantiate her claims, she also uses pathos to support her argument.

The emotional aspect of Tan's essay is clear. Witness her statement that she had difficulty with standardized testing because her response to the questions tended to dovetail with her emotional reaction to the ideas suggested, such as those of "sunset" and "nightfall." Here and throughout the essay, she appeals to her audience's sense of humor, as when she describes pretending to be her mother on the phone in order to get a better response to a business enquiry; even more powerfully, she garners our sympathy for her mother's concern about her medical situation, and the sense of frustration inherent in the resulting dilemma, in which the doctor's dismissing of the patient (Tan's mother) seems to trump taking the trouble to simply communicate with her.

Thus, Amy Tan employs ethical, logical, and emotional strategies to convey her cautionary argument about the importance of clear communication. Without an awareness of how we are coming across to our readers, without a reexamination of our preconceived ideas, without a sense of how we sound to that one key person sitting in the "audience" as we project our words from the stage, we risk losing an all-important connection. Instead of struggling to find the most impressive way to express our ideas, instead of always trying to be successful in ways we let other people define for us, perhaps we should be focusing on our most important task as human beings, communication, and searching to find our true language, our best language, our "mother tongue."

Here is a review of the process to follow as you attempt this task

- Read the document carefully, with a view to understanding and critiquing it

- Introduce/give an overview or summary

- Create a thesis about the aspects of the document you plan to examine

- Develop body paragraphs, each one about a distinct aspect of the document; use quotations from the author to substantiate your interpretation

- Conclude by reaffirming your thesis and considering the broader implications of the discussion

- Give your paper a title, ideally indicating the author/essay and your approach to the materials

Review Exercise: Analyze This! Choose an Essay from the Cited Readings

Write a Rhetorical Analysis of one of our readings:

—Title should indicate author and focus

—Intro must mention full name of author and document

—Give an overview of the argument

—Lead into your thesis, which is about the author's use of ethos (appealing to our sense of ethics, what is right and wrong), pathos (appealing to our emotions, evoking sympathy, and/or empathy), and logos (using logic) in attempting to persuade the audience

—Last sentence of your intro must say that the author uses ethos, pathos, and logos to convey the argument

—Have one paragraph each regarding the author's use of the various rhetorical strategies: one mentioning ethos, one mentioning pathos, one mentioning logos; each paragraph should contain at least one direct quotation

—Close with a reaffirmation of your thesis (mentioning author's use of ethos, pathos, and logos), followed by a consideration of the broader social implications of the topic

—You do not need to give page numbers for your quotes, but you do need to fit them smoothly and logically into your sentence structures

Your essay should be several pages long (double-spaced). Do not use secondary sources.

Please edit carefully for all aspects of grammar and writing style.

RHETORICAL ANALYSIS ESSAY

AUTHOR	ARTICLE

TITLE:

INTRODUCTION

ETHOS

PATHS

PATHOS

LOGOS

CONCLUSION

WRITING RESEARCH ESSAYS—
Charting the Journey

One of the fundamental skills you need to master as a university student is writing a research paper, so let's start with an overview of the process. In some of your courses, you will have a set topic or selection of topics—or you may have an open choice. Regardless of your subject area, you will have the task of exploring ideas of interest, reading through a variety of source materials (typically not provided for you—you'll need to find them yourself in most cases), developing an argument about the subject, and synthesizing your research into a coherent discussion.

While some other types of essays you write at university will permit (or even encourage) the inclusion of personal material, a research paper is unlikely to do so, as it requires an objective rather than a subjective approach. What will be uniquely yours about the essay is the approach you take to the material and the way in which you integrate the sources into the discussion.

Scholarly work necessarily rests on the shoulders of those intellectuals who have come before us: the experts in any given field to whom we turn for enlightenment and inspiration. So how do we choose our sources for inclusion in our argument?

Commonsense guidelines can help steer us through the selection process. As we incorporate selected ideas into our essay as sources, we need to ensure that we do so in a logical—and ethical—way. Some courses will require the use of scholarly sources only, such as peer-reviewed journals. It is always a good idea to check with your instructor regarding the acceptability of sources of various types.

Academic integrity is essential, so be sure to use your moral compass when you embark on this intellectual journey! Integral to this will be the skills of annotation, citation, and bibliography. Documentation format, be it in Modern Language Association (MLA), American Psychological Association (APA), Chicago Style, or another method, is a challenging but crucial component of the final copy of your paper to be submitted for evaluation. Remember, details matter!

So, are you ready to write a research paper? To get you started, we will look at some aspects of research, at the introductory level and beyond, which are essential to the process. You can apply these skills in this class as well as other university courses. First, we will think about the experience and attitudes we bring to the task; then, as we proceed through the phases of planning a project and implementing the outline, we will make sure that we know how to avoid some of the potential pitfalls of writing this type of essay.

We will also consider the practical tasks of debating, presenting ideas to the rest of the class in an oral report, and the details of editing that are particularly important. Ideally, a research paper is an opportunity for you as a student not only to find out more about a subject of interest, but to exercise your ability to put ideas together into a compelling argument on the subject.

Whatever the topic, make it your passion project!

Discussion and Writing Opportunity: Formulating a Research Topic

Choose one of the following questions and write an essay of 300–400 words (four to five equal paragraphs including an introduction and conclusion).

1. If you had the option to choose any subject you are interested in as the topic for a research paper, what would you choose and why? You may use first-person singular "I" in this essay.

    OR

2. Can you recall an essay you wrote sometime in the past that required you to use secondary sources? Discuss your experience of researching and writing (use first-person singular "I" to do so), and consider the ways in which you could improve your process next time.

    OR

3. What are the most important steps and strategies for writing a paper requiring research? You may use first-person singular "I" to discuss your experience.

Jot down a few ideas before you begin . . .

Now, write out your answer in the form of a brief essay, with a title reflecting your choice among the three questions:

As always, read through what you have written and make any changes you wish before sharing this essay.

Choosing Research Sources: "No Wikipedia" and Beyond

In evaluating and making use of research sources, to determine the usefulness of a source, we can consider some evaluative questions. Who seems to be the target audience? Rather than defaulting to the idea of the general public, try considering aspects of demographics such as age, culture, education, and so on. Who (besides your instructor or fellow students) would be most interested in reading your essay?

You should also consider whether your instructor requires a variety of types of sources, for example, a minimum number of books, journal articles, and so forth. Does your instructor permit the use of websites? Blogs? Videos? Interviews? News reports? and so forth.

Is the source primarily expository (imparting information, as is the case for Wikipedia or any encyclopedic source) or persuasive (making an argument)? Note that wiki sources are by nature open to amendment, and therefore subject to change (thus dangerous from a research point of view—hence, many instructors have a "no Wikipedia" rule).

On the other hand, such articles do provide useful, general information and often have links to bona fide sources, so you can certainly look at those sources themselves and then cite from them directly if they prove useful. The main issue with any -pedia source is that it is giving information rather than analysis, argument, or critique. You want to look beyond the facts.

If a source's aim is persuasive, how does it make use of ethos (ethics), pathos (emotion), and/or logos (logic)? If the focus is logical, is it inductive (reasoning inward toward a general conclusion) or deductive (reasoning outward from a general idea)?

Do you see any fallacies (errors in logic), such as the following . . .?

Hasty generalization (insufficient evidence to support the conclusion)

Post hoc ergo propter hoc (chronological sequence masquerading as logical sequence)

Red herring (going off in the wrong direction due to misleading and irrelevant data)

Ad hominem (using the personal rather than the logical as the basis for argument)

Ad populum (appealing to the masses)

Using Secondary Sources

Inherent in the nature of a research paper is the use and proper acknowledgment of secondary sources. You may well find that the rules in postsecondary institutions are likely to be more rigorous than those at the high school level (unless your secondary school had very strict rules to begin with).

To state it simply, any ideas that do not come from your own thoughts (when in doubt, err on the side of caution) require such recognition—and failure to do so will land you with a charge of academic dishonesty, cheating, or plagiarism, which will have serious consequences for your future in academic life and beyond. Sometimes, cheating is the result of a lack of confidence in one's own abilities. Don't let your insecurities guide you down this treacherous path.

Standard penalties include a grade of zero for the assignment for the first offense. A second offense typically results in failure of the course. Upon a third offense, in the same course or another course, a permanent notation of academic dishonesty becomes part of the student's official records from the institution.

It is simply not worth the risk of compromising your future to violate the rules for documenting your sources properly, so let's take some time to think about ways in which you might deliberately—or unintentionally—go off the rails. Note that a claim of ignorance of the rules ("I didn't realize"), or of forgetting them, will not be considered excuses or mitigating factors.

Getting too much help is a form of cheating as well; having someone else write your paper (paid or unpaid) is an obvious violation, but even a substantial edit or revision that is essentially a rewrite is also called plagiarism, in that you are representing someone else's writing as your own.

Even recycling your own essays from other courses is a problem, unless you acknowledge your source—which begs the question, "Couldn't you find a better source than your own work?" If in doubt, ask your professor for guidance.

It is your responsibility as a student to be aware of these rules, just as it is your responsibility as a citizen to be aware of laws. A famous skit by comedian Steve Martin is based on the idea of using forgetfulness as an excuse; he uses the example of a thief who gets caught by the police and offers his defense as follows: "***I forgot*** armed robbery is illegal." Good luck with that!

To get back to the world of essay writing, most people know, for instance, that cutting and pasting material from somewhere (e.g. online) constitutes an act of cheating unless the material is in quotation marks and the source is cited properly in the bibliographical list at the end of the document.

In fact, acknowledging sources may be easier than you think—it only takes a minute, and it could save your academic career.

Avoiding Plagiarism, Starting with an Original Outline

Taking a close look at the rubric for grading research papers, we can see the importance of ensuring that you document your sources scrupulously: plagiarism, which is the result of having inadequate or missing references, will automatically lead to a failing grade. Of course, getting someone else to write your paper, online or in person, is also a clear form of cheating and a violation of academic integrity.

Again, the concept is fairly simple and straightforward: any source from which you take material must have an in-text citation and a Works Cited entry. Every source on the Works Cited list must be actually cited in-text, and any in-text citation must also appear in the list at the end. Failure to do so, for instance if you had no in-text citations but only a bibliography at the end, is in itself a violation of the guidelines for academic honesty at the postsecondary level, and is likely to result in a failing grade as a minimum penalty.

Remember, getting someone else to write your paper, getting too much editing help from a tutor or someone else, and recycling an essay from another course are other forms of cheating that garner harsh penalties. The best way to ensure originality is to begin with a clear structure for the unique discussion you are putting together, the bones you will flesh out with properly acknowledged material from your research sources.

You may begin with an outline reflecting the ideas you plan to explore, and then modify the outline based on the research you do. Here is an example of such an outline—note that it does not include specific references to sources, or quotes. (Some outline assignments may require a bibliography.)

Term Paper Outline: The Unsettling Truth behind Artificial Intelligence

Thesis: Although artificial intelligence (AI) may increase efficiency for organizations that use it, the replacement of natural intelligence with a manufactured form results in the decline of human beings' everyday individual skills, the inability to think and speak based on one's own opinions and values, and the intensified disconnection of our society today.

I. The decline of basic everyday skills and abilities is the inevitable result of using AI.

   A. With AI, people do not have to work on their own.

   B. With robotic machines to do everyday work and chores, people do not need to practice these skills.

II. The inability to speak and think for oneself is dissolving.

   A. Individuals already look toward the internet to find answers quickly and efficiently.

   B. People do not put much thought into their actions.

III. Intensified disconnection of our society today will result from AI.

   A. AI can lead to human insecurities.

   B. Knowing that machines are capable of performing better than human beings may lead them to a lack of ambition.

Note the use of Roman numerals for main ideas and the use of capital letters for subordinate ideas. Subsequent levels of subordination would require regular numbers (1, 2), then small letters (a, b), then small Roman numerals (i, ii). The more detailed the outline, the easier the process of writing the essay itself will be (though we still need not include details such as quotes and sources in the outline document, typically).

Remember that the minimum number of points at each level is two; hence, no A without B, no 1 without 2, and so forth. This rule is based on the logical premise that if you divide something into parts, the minimum number of parts you can have is two. Now, try putting together your own outline for a research topic of interest to you, bearing in mind that you can increase the number of points at any level, and that you can adapt the outline in a later version to reflect any changes that seem necessary in light of your research.

RESEARCH ESSAY OUTLINE

TITLE:

TOPIC:

THESIS:

I.

A.

B.

II.

A.

B.

III.

A.

B.

Annotations, Citations, and Bibliographies

The process of proper documentation necessarily begins during the research phase. You need to take careful notes (and not just mental notes) of everything you read. Who said it? Where (precisely which source)? Is it an exact quote? Unless you can answer these questions, you are precluded from using the material at all!

Not sure how to cite? You can type the documentation style and the type of document to which you are referring (e.g., "MLA citation documentary film") into your search engine to find the up-to-date requirements and contemporary examples. In the MLA system of documentation, we use parenthetical in-text citations (bracketed acknowledgment of source materials, such as with a surname and page number) in tandem with an alphabetical list of Works Cited at the end of the document. (Alternate methods, such as Chicago Style, use footnotes and a list of References).

The key concept here is that you are dexterously and conscientiously weaving into your argument materials that come from various sources that are relevant and appropriate. The argument is substantiated and developed by means of the cited materials.

At any point in the process of writing your research paper, if you need help finding materials, remember that librarians are a rich source of advice and practical help. Do not rely solely on the method of typing keywords into your search engine—visit a local library in person and talk to the person at the information desk. No doubt, they will have some suggestions not only regarding where and how to find sources, but can also direct you to some detailed guidelines on documentation protocols.

You can also look at and use citation sites such as <u>NoodleTools</u> and <u>EasyBib</u> to help with this process. For example, here is a citation of this book in MLA format:

Blenkhorn, Deborah. *Introduction to Academic Reading and Writing Skills for University Students.*
   Kendall Hunt, 2019.

Note that we cannot use information from any website or published book unless we give the author (or site) credit—both inside our text and at the end of our paper. In other words, it is not enough to simply list at the end of your document the sources you have used.

As your instructor reads your essay, he or she should clearly be able to see which sentences, facts, or sections of your essay came from Source A, Source B, or Source C, and so forth, by looking at your in-text citations.

Whether quoting directly or paraphrasing (and note that in academic writing, we do not want to use quotes unless actually quoting), you will need a parenthetical reference. The basic principle is to use the author's last name and page number (Jones 35), unless the author's identity is already clear from context, for example, mentioned in your sentence, in which case you would need just the page number (35). Note that this system does not use footnotes for bibliographic details; instead, we see full details in the alphabetized Works Cited list at the end of the document.

The cited material needs to fit smoothly and logically into your sentence structure. Each sentence in your document, whether it contains cited material or not, needs to be grammatically correct and stylistically appropriate in terms of formality, conciseness, and professionalism.

As a general rule, paraphrase your sources whenever you believe that you can make the information from a source clearer for your audience by using your own words. Use direct quotations only when you feel that the original wording is somehow unique and distinctive. (Note, as a general rule, do not use quotation marks unless you are actually quoting.) In incorporating your sources into your essay, remember that quotes cannot stand alone—they cannot be placed in a sentence all by themselves.

You need to make each quote a part of your essay by introducing it beforehand and commenting on it afterward. Ideally, quotes within each paragraph will come from alternating sources (rather than multiple subsequent quotes from the same source). Again, this strategy has a significant impact on the coherence of your document.

An effective technique for ensuring that you keep track of where you get your ideas from when you are preparing your essay using secondary sources is to keep careful notes when you are researching. Many options are available to you, beyond simply making a mental note (you cannot count on being able to recall details at a later date).

Some students like to use cue cards, lined or unlined rectangles of stiff paper, which we can initially use as bookmarks, then record data in point form if we decide to use the source material.

Note: you can use these templates for making your own cue cards to keep track of the important details of your research.

Remember, each documentation style has its own protocols, and each type of source within that documentation style is subject to particular requirements: input the source type and the documentation style into your search engine for up-to-date examples; make sure your research notes contain all of the information you need to cite.

RESEARCH NOTES

(Always check with your instructor which documentation style you will be using: MLA, APA, Chicago Style, etc.)

SOURCE:
BIBLIOGRAPHIC DETAILS:
IDEAS:
DIRECTLY QUOTED MATERIAL:

SOURCE:
BIBLIOGRAPHIC DETAILS:
IDEAS:
DIRECTLY QUOTED MATERIAL:

SOURCE:

BIBLIOGRAPHIC DETAILS:

IDEAS:

DIRECTLY QUOTED MATERIAL:

SOURCE:

BIBLIOGRAPHIC DETAILS:

IDEAS:

DIRECTLY QUOTED MATERIAL:

When to Use and Not to Use the Personal Approach: Debates and Presentations

Although a research paper requires objectivity, without an intrinsic personal connection to your topic you may find it difficult to spark and maintain your interest in your essay. If your research topic is truly a passion project, the challenge may be to keep your passions in check while you navigate the process of putting together a well-reasoned essay.

To prepare for the experience of arguing your position logically in your paper, one useful step is to debate the issue. Debating is a worthwhile exercise in that, while you may support one side of an argument instinctively and unilaterally, you will be forced to consider the topic from an alternate point of view.

Debates can be formal (as you may have seen in the proceedings of a formal debating club at school, or a televised political debate between candidates for an elected office) or informal (as in an impromptu discussion in which people take opposing sides on an issue).

A semiformal debate in class, as part of the process for preparing to write a research paper, can offer a relatively casual opportunity to explore the PROs and CONs ("pro" is Latin for "for"; "con" is Latin for "against") and to get some feedback from your peers and your instructor. An in-class debate will require at least two presenters, one for each side of the argument.

To prepare for the debate, all group members need to cooperate to formulate the initial statement:

BE IT RESOLVED THAT _____.

The group will need to come up with points on both sides, decide who will say what, and plan a presentation according to the given structure. A sample structure for a semiformal debate, with a total presentation time of less than ten minutes, is as follows:

INTRODUCTION OF TOPIC AND PRESENTERS

PRO: two minutes

CON: two minutes

PRO (REBUTTAL): one minute

CON (REBUTTAL): one minute

CONCLUSION, QUESTION PERIOD, AND CLASS VOTE (SECRET BALLOT)

During the debate presentation, although you may convey enthusiasm for the point of view you are articulating, you need to maintain professionalism and an atmosphere of mutual respect among classmates.

Calling your opponents or their arguments "stupid" would be an obvious example of violating these principles—but any insult, slander, or mockery, whether subtle or overt, is out of line. An appropriate tone is a key component that will also come through for you in the writing process later.

Maintaining eye contact with your audience and your fellow presenters is always a good idea in order to ensure engagement and understanding. Try speaking at measured pace (relatively slow compared to conversation), and in a fairly low register (again, more so than you would in talking casually). Project your voice sufficiently to reach the back of the room, without overdoing it.

Body language can help with voice projection, as slouching may lead to mumbling; standing up straight with your arms comfortably at your sides (or holding your note cards, etc.) will naturally allow you to vocalize more effectively.

If nerves are a factor, make sure you have reasonably done all you can to minimize anxiety. Know your material thoroughly, and practice aloud before the event. You don't need to dress any particular way—but a good rule to keep in mind is that your appearance should not distract your listeners in any way from what you have to say.

While you may have with you some brief notes to consult (a particularly good idea if you are afraid you may forget something), avoid reading from a prepared script in order to make your delivery seem fresh and spontaneous. When it is someone else's turn to speak, give that person your full attention, showing the same respect you would like to receive in return.

Good timing is usually more than good luck—chances are you will need to adjust the amount of material you have to present in light of how long it takes to say it out loud at a reasonable pace. Trying to get through extra material at an increased speed is risky—you may lose coherence and audience attention if you do so. Practicing aloud, with a timer, is the best way to ensure that you are within the given parameters.

What will you do with the legitimate points that contradict your thesis? One suggestion is to put them into your introduction (or at least early in your paper) as a concession, then follow swiftly with a rebuttal. For instance, in his 1948 essay, "Politics and the English Language," George Orwell begins with a statement about the commonly held view that language is on its own evolutionary path, which reflects a declining society, and which we cannot change—then he quickly proceeds to his thesis that "the process is reversible."

NOTE: While the research essay itself will not make use of first-person "I," you may have the opportunity to present your project to your fellow students. When you talk about your research and your process of formulating the argument, you may consider the personal interests informing your focus on the topic, and the steps you are taking to explore it.

DEBATE EVALUATION FORM   Topic:

Names of Group Members Presenting the Debate:

_____

	NEEDS TO IMPROVE	ALMOST SUFFICIENT	ADEQUATE	ABOVE AVERAGE	EXCELLENT
CONTENT (IDEAS)					
SPEAKING (CLARITY)					
TIMING (LENGTH)					
EYE CONTACT					
BODY LANGUAGE					

Vote for PRO or CON? (Circle one).

DEBATE EVALUATION FORM   Topic:

Names of Group Members Presenting the Debate:

_____

	NEEDS TO IMPROVE	ALMOST SUFFICIENT	ADEQUATE	ABOVE AVERAGE	EXCELLENT
CONTENT (IDEAS)					
SPEAKING (CLARITY)					
TIMING (LENGTH)					
EYE CONTACT					
BODY LANGUAGE					

Vote for PRO or CON? (Circle one).

DEBATE EVALUATION FORM   Topic:

Names of Group Members Presenting the Debate:

_____

	NEEDS TO IMPROVE	ALMOST SUFFICIENT	ADEQUATE	ABOVE AVERAGE	EXCELLENT
CONTENT (IDEAS)					
SPEAKING (CLARITY)					
TIMING (LENGTH)					
EYE CONTACT					
BODY LANGUAGE					

Vote for PRO or CON? (Circle one).

DEBATE EVALUATION FORM   Topic:

Names of Group Members Presenting the Debate:

_____

	NEEDS TO IMPROVE	ALMOST SUFFICIENT	ADEQUATE	ABOVE AVERAGE	EXCELLENT
CONTENT (IDEAS)					
SPEAKING (CLARITY)					
TIMING (LENGTH)					
EYE CONTACT					
BODY LANGUAGE					

Vote for PRO or CON? (Circle one).

RESEARCH PRESENTATION

—Introduce yourself (print your name here; you will hand in this sheet)

Hello, my name is _____

—Complete the following statements:

I am doing my Term Paper on the topic of

_____

My thesis is

_____

_____

_____

My body paragraphs will be about

_____

_____

_____

_____

_____

_____

_____

_____

_____

Sources I will cite include the following:

_____
_____
_____
_____
_____
_____
_____
_____
_____
_____

I chose this topic because

_____
_____
_____
_____
_____
_____
_____

—Ask if there are any questions from the audience.

—Thank the audience for their attention.

Protocols for Citation and Document Format

We can see online many representations of document format for formal academic essays, especially by, for instance, googling "MLA Research Paper Images." Since not all of those representations are accurate or up to date, you may wish to ensure you are looking at something from a reputable site such as Purdue OWL. Here is an MLA-style essay template on the subject of MLA Essays, followed by a detailed grading rubric:

Your Name

Professor

Course and Section Number

Due Date

Assignment Type, for example, Research Essay

In writing an MLA style paper, be sure to start with the proper format. Font and spacing must be consistent throughout the document. Each paragraph is a standard tab indent. No extra space occurs between paragraphs. All paragraphs are approximately the same length. Start with a hook, something relevant to the topic that grabs the reader's attention. Lead in from the hook to the thesis, which is the main argument for the paper. A good thesis does the following: makes an argument about the topic (must be debatable), does not ask a question, and foregrounds the body of the essay by means of keywords. It is about the topic, not about the paper itself. Do not use first-person singular to talk about opinions, feelings, beliefs, and so forth. Do not talk about what the paper will do: just do it.

As you develop your research paper, note that the body paragraphs should contain examples and quotations that prove the thesis. Specifics come from cited research rather than personal knowledge and experience. Putting together the paragraphs, remember that coherence is important within the paper as a whole. Avoid transitions of chronology (unless actually talking about a sequential process); instead, think of logical connections between ideas. Think about transitions as ways of getting from one idea to the next with a smooth flow. When subdividing the argument, remember that we usually need three body paragraphs or more, in addition to the introduction and conclusion. We should see at least one paragraph break per typed page, and no more than two paragraph breaks. The standard is about one third to one half a page of double spaced typing; approximately 125 words. Sentences will be a variety of lengths and structures; perhaps we will have several per paragraph, as a rough guide.

Within our sentences, the words we choose will be suitable for academic writing. Check each sentence for a clear subject and a strong verb. Sentences beginning with "There" or "It" plus the verb "to be" do not fulfill this requirement. Similarly, passive voice is less effective than active voice (in active voice, the subject performs the action of the verb). In terms of diction, avoid vague words such as "thing," "big," "a lot," and so forth. Informal language also requires editing: words such as "kids," "TV," "mom and dad," and so forth. Political correctness is also a factor: avoid gender-specific language, as well as racial or cultural slurs. Whenever we use "this," we need a specific noun directly afterward. Second-person pronoun use is nonstandard for academic papers.

Having edited carefully, we can consider the conclusion of our paper. We begin with a reaffirmation of the thesis (reworded), but do not repeat the specifics covered earlier in the essay. Instead, broaden the discussion outward to consider more general consequences or implications of the essay you have written, the issue you are exploring. Think about humanity as a whole, the larger picture, or the future. Consider positive and/or negative outcomes. Aim for something profound and thought provoking. Leave the reader with a strong impression. A final edit is essential to ensure submission of the best possible work.

(Add Works Cited at the end, starting on a separate page, for your research paper)

Note, this rubric for a research paper in an English class is based on a system of 20 criteria: 10 for content and 10 for expression. This division of values reflects the importance of assessing a balance between what you say and how you say it.

RUBRIC FOR RESEARCH ESSAYS

CONTENT

0	1	2	3	4
— No hook	— Relevance of hook unclear	— Hook is too generic (definition of well-known term; "In society today . . ."; author birthdate, etc.)	— Insufficient lead-in between hook and thesis	— Effective hook, leading coherently into the thesis statement
— No thesis is readily apparent	— "Thesis" phrased as a question rather than a statement	— Thesis not sufficiently debatable (not an argument)	— Thesis not sufficient to foreground the body paragraphs	— Suitable thesis (arguable and anticipatory)
— No citations (automatic F)	— Inconsistency between citations and works cited list	— Citations not in proper and consistent format	— Citation sources lack smooth integration (e.g., consecutive citing of same source)	— In-text citations in proper format in each body para, corresponding to works cited page
— Direct reference to the essay itself as such	— Discussion less about the topic than about the paper itself	— Reference to forthcoming or previous material in the document itself	— Chronological transitions, referring only to the order of points within the document	— No self-referential wording to the document itself
— Praise of author or work(s)	— Opinion rather than analysis of the material	— Cited praise of author or work(s), rather than analytical commentary	— Subtle or implied praise of author or work(s)	— No praise of author or work(s)
— Use of first-person pronoun "I"	— Reference to the student's first-person experience (without using "I")	— Use of "I" in quoted material (should be altered with square brackets to a noun or pronoun)	— Improperly executed or awkward attempt(s) to avoid "I"	— No first-person singular content

0	1	2	3	4
— Frequent and widespread use of second-person pronoun "you"	— Occasional use of "you"	— Use of "you" in quotations (use square brackets to change to a noun or pronoun)	— single instance of "you" in essay	— No second-person pronoun use
— Failure to use literary present tense where necessary	— Inconsistent use of appropriate tense (sometimes correct; sometimes incorrect)	— Inappropriate use of present tense, for example, for past historical details external to the work	— Use of past tense instead of present perfect where necessary	— Appropriate use of literary present, including present perfect where necessary
— Lacking connections between ideas	— Inconsistent or somewhat illogical use of transitions	— Connections of addition ("another," etc.)	— Attempts at transitional phrasing, but still somewhat awkward	— Clear and coherent links between ideas
— No conclusion	— Conclusion too generic (fails to reaffirm the thesis before expanding the ideas)	— Conclusion too repetitive (too much restatement of previous material)	— Conclusion lacking effective development (too short; lacking reaffirmation of thesis; ends abruptly, etc.)	— Appropriate closure, beginning with a reworded reaffirmation of the thesis and broadening to consider the implications . . .

EXPRESSION

0	1	2	3	4
— One grammatical error or more per sentence	— Basic errors such as those of subject–verb agreement, preposition idiom, article use, and verb form	— Only occasional errors resulting from oral speech patterns (common mistakes)	— Only a few minor grammatical inconsistencies in the entire document	— Grammatically correct prose
— Sentence structure errors in most sentences throughout the document	— Run-ons and/or fragments, mixed constructions, dangling or misplaced modifiers in every paragraph	— Approximately 50% of sentences have effective structures and proper punctuation	— Only a few sentences that would benefit from clearer and more coherent construction in the entire document	— Effective sentence structures
— Slang/informal language/jargon/clichés appear often	— Inappropriate diction in every paragraph	— Evidence of attempts to edit for appropriate style	— Only a few minor lapses in diction	— Consistently formal, academic/professional style
— Passive and/or expletive constructions creating grammatical errors	— Passives and/or expletives in every paragraph	— Passive or weak expletive constructions (but not both) in every paragraph	— Only very occasional use of passive voice and weak expletives	— Avoidance of unnecessary passive voice, as well as weak sentence structures with "there" or "it" (as a vague pronoun) + to be
— No proper punctuation patterns with cited material	— Citation errors in every paragraph	— Some evidence of citation protocols (e.g., 50% correct)	— Very few inconsistencies in incorporating cited materials	— Cited materials coherently incorporated into the discussion

0	1	2	3	4
— Proofreading errors throughout the document; inconsistent font (including size and no bold)	— Proofreading errors in every paragraph	— Some evidence of editing for mechanical errors	— Only rare slips in spelling and minor "typos," and so forth	— Font consistent; spelling correct; transcription errors fixed; no words missing, and so forth
— Spacing is not set to "double"	— Spacing is set to double for part of the document only	— Extra space between paragraphs but otherwise correct	— Extra space after title and works cited heading only	— Spacing is consistently double
— Title specs and headers are missing	— Title specs or headers are missing, but not both	— Minor errors in title specs and headers	— Minor errors in title specs or headers, but not both	— Title specs and headers are correct
— No margins and no indents	— Indents or margins are missing, but not both	— Minor errors in indents and margins	— Minor errors in indents or margins, but not both	— Margins and indents are correct
— No Works Cited list (automatic F)	— Not in alphabetical order	— Significant deviation from protocols	— Minor errors or inconsistencies	— Appropriate Works Cited list

Review Exercise: Documentation Dilemmas

Exchange a draft of your completed research paper with a peer (or exchange among a group of three). You may select whom you work with on the basis of topic, compatibility, and/or writing level. (Sometimes, the instructor may choose to set up partnerships or groups for an exercise of this type).

Go through the preceding rubric for research essays and give your partner targeted feedback for editing by circling or highlighting the appropriate sections. Add a general comment at the end (aim for constructive criticism) to reflect your overall impression, along with a total score for the paper as a whole. Be fair, and be realistic! If in doubt, as always, check in with your instructor.

Having gone through all of these stages, you should be ready to submit your own research paper to your instructor for evaluation.

Good luck with your writing and editing process!

SECTION 6
EDITING—
Fine-Tuning Your Work

As any good writer will tell you, one of the most challenging and rewarding parts of the composition process is maximizing the impact of your writing through the application of targeted editing strategies. In any genre or type of writing, we can push the boundaries of style to venture into new creative territory, opening ourselves up to the possibility of critical evaluation by readers who may find the unconventional either exciting or confusing—or both! When we revise our work, analogous to the process of fine-tuning in the world of music, we do not want to take away what makes the work unique, yet we also need to be aware of what it takes to ensure that our audience finds what we have to present to them to be appealing, appropriate, and accessible.

At the level of grammar and sentence construction, we may choose to experiment with levels of correctness (for instance, we may choose to use sentence fragments deliberately to represent a theme of fragmentation) and formality (for instance, we may choose the informality of contractions [can't, etc.] over a more professional or academic approach [cannot, etc.]). The advisability of such a strategy is limited in formal contexts, of course. Yet the connection between form and function is something we can be constantly aware of both as readers and writers: a valuable exercise is to take a look at a writer whose work you admire, to consider this form–function connection. Just remember, an established has more leeway than does an aspiring student.

One hallmark of the writing of well-known practitioners of style is imagery; if we do not have any imagery in the first draft of our document, we may consider adding it in to our edited version. The more specific the imagery, the better: the reader needs to be able to imagine perception through one or more of the five senses (two or more at the same time is synesthesia). Categories of concrete sensory detail are as follows. Examples?

Visual _____

Auditory _____

Olfactory _____

Gustatory _____

Tactile/kinesthetic _____

Tone also has much to do with the way in which the writer (or speaker in the piece) comes across to the audience, which may or may not be an accurate reflection of that writer's true thoughts or feelings. (Note that "mood" as distinguished from tone is how we as readers feel in response.) The writer may speak in his or her own voice—but that limitation is context-specific.

Try to be aware of how your tone is coming across to your readers, and edit to ensure you are successfully conveying it. For example, Jonathan Swift notoriously wrote ostensibly as an advocate of cannibalism—to make a satirical point about social responsibility.

When we are editing, we want to start at the level of content, which includes aspects of imagery and tone, as well as logic and overall structure: this initial stage is called *macro editing*, and we need to spend some time doing so before we proceed to the *micro editing* phase. After all, to change the details of wording something that may require drastic alteration would be a potential waste of time.

When we are satisfied at the level of ideas, we can proceed to check for aspects of grammar and writing style. This step is critical—even if you are in an in-class writing situation.

Don't get carried away by your own momentum!

For an effective edit even when you are short on time, try proofreading your work backward, for example, start at the last sentence of your conclusion, then read the second-last sentence, third-last sentence, and so on.

This strategy interrupts the continuity of your thought process, which can otherwise distract you from grammar and sentence structure if you read only from start to finish.

Following, you will see a checklist of aspects of style to consider when editing. Look through one of your previous writing assignments from this or another class, and create your own personal checklist in light of these ten tips.

You can add other checklist items as well. Looking ahead to the "Ten Commandments of Style" may provide some further ideas for revision strategies.

You may also wish to consider comments and feedback you have received on your writing in the past—in English class or in other courses you have taken over the years.

For each checklist item that you create on your own personal chart, give an example from your own writing, and add an editing suggestion (a revised version of your original phrasing).

Then, the next time you are editing your work, think about the personal checklist you have created.

CHECKLIST: TEN TIPS ON STYLE TO CONSIDER WHEN EDITING

1. "This"
   - Always add a noun after the word "this" for clarity

2. "There"
   - Replace the word "there" + a form of the verb "to be" with a stronger subject–verb combination

3. "It"
   - Use the pronoun "it" only to refer specifically to a previous noun

4. "A lot"/"big"
   - Consider more sophisticated alternative phrasing to amplify ideas

5. "Thing"
   - Find a noun to express a precise meaning

6. Passive voice
   - Change to active voice, so that the subject of the sentence performs the action of the verb

7. Contractions
   - Write out full forms, for example, "will not" instead of "won't."

8. Informality
   - Choose words that are less colloquial, for example, "children" rather than "kids"; "man" rather than "guy."

9. Idiom
   - Commit to memory any Standard English expressions that seem new or unusual

10. Political correctness
    - Avoid gender-specific (e.g., "mankind") and outdated terminology (e.g., "third world")

Discussion and Writing Opportunity: Creating a Targeted Checklist

CHECKLIST ITEM	EXAMPLE	CORRECTION

CHECKLIST ITEM	EXAMPLE	CORRECTION

Proofreading Strategies

Here is a sample rubric indicating areas to be aware of when proofreading an essay:

0	1	2	3	4
— Off-topic (automatic F)	— Body paragraph topics overlap or do not relate clearly to thesis	— Generally on-topic, but with some significant discrepancies	— Not clearly on-topic in only one minor instance	— On-topic, that is, a direct answer to the essay question
— No thesis is readily apparent	— "Thesis" phrased as a question rather than a statement	— Thesis not sufficiently debatable (not an argument)	— Thesis not sufficient to foreground the body paragraphs	— Hook leading into suitable thesis (arguable and anticipatory)
— Direct reference to the essay itself as such	— Discussion less about the topic than about the paper itself	— Reference to forthcoming or previous material in the document itself	— Chronological wording referring only to the order of points within the document	— No self-referential wording to the document itself
— No paragraph divisions apparent in the document	— Inconsistent and/or inadequate development of body paragraphs	— Some evidence of editing for paragraph development, but significant inconsistencies still apparent	— Minor inconsistencies in paragraph development	— Adequate development of balanced paragraphs in the body of the essay, including specific and relevant examples that prove the thesis
— Lacking connections between ideas	— Inconsistent or somewhat illogical use of transitions	— Connections of addition ("another," etc.)	— Attempts at transitional phrasing, but still somewhat awkward	— Clear and coherent links between ideas
— No conclusion	— Conclusion too generic (fails to reaffirm the thesis before expanding the ideas)	— Conclusion too repetitive (too much restatement of previous material)	— Conclusion lacking effective development (too short; lacking reaffirmation of thesis; ends abruptly, etc.)	— Appropriate closure, beginning with a reworded reaffirmation of the thesis and broadening to implications ...

0	1	2	3	4
— One grammatical error or more per sentence (automatic F)	— Basic errors such as those of subject–verb agreement, preposition idiom, article use, and verb form	— Only occasional errors resulting from oral speech patterns (common mistakes)	— Only a few minor grammatical inconsistencies in the entire document	— Grammatically correct prose
— Sentence structure errors in most sentences throughout the document	— Run-ons and/or fragments, mixed constructions, dangling or misplaced modifiers in every paragraph	— Approximately 50% of sentences have effective structures and proper punctuation	— Only a few sentences that would benefit from clearer and more coherent construction in the entire document	— Effective sentence structures
— Slang/informal language/jargon/clichés in many sentences	— Inappropriate diction in every paragraph	— Evidence of attempts to edit for appropriate style	— Only a few minor lapses in diction	— Consistently formal, academic/professional style
— Vague and/or wordy use of language in every paragraph	— Some use of either "this"/"it" as vague references, or use of sentence structures with "there" + to be, or unnecessary use of passive voice	— Approximately 50% of document avoids vague and wordy patterns of expression	— A few minor instances of vague or wordy patterns	— Precise and accurate diction
— Transcription errors; little or no evidence of editing; document format errors	— Overall impression that student did not observe format requirements or edit for transcription errors	— Some evidence of editing, but further proofreading required	— Only minor editing issues	— Evidence of careful editing; margins; double-spacing and clear indentation of each paragraph

Academic/Professional Writing Style: Avoiding Colloquialisms, Slang, Clichés, Vague, and Informal Language

A.K.A. THE TEN COMMANDMENTS OF STYLE . . . BABY!

As we get started with the editing process, one of the key concepts to understand is as follows: every writing experience has a context, and every context has a norm. So, what you say (content) and how you say it (style) will vary depending on where you say it (context) and to whom you say it (audience). When we mix these up, we get something funny (which could be funny in the sense of "odd" and/or funny in the sense of "humorous"). One would assume you raised your eyebrows (perhaps literally or just metaphorically) at the abbreviation "a.k.a." and put the word "baby" (with an exclamation point, no less) into the title of our lecture.

Your sense of surprise most likely came from the unexpectedness of the use of colloquialism in what is ostensibly (a handy academic word, meaning "supposedly") a formal writing situation. Why do it, then? Well, to get your attention (baby!) and to make a point. (If the "funny" part still isn't clear, try watching a Woody Allen film called *Bananas*—if you watch it, you'll see the "audience" scene in question—not for those who are easily offended!)

One of the goals for this course is to show you some guidelines for writing that may be unfamiliar at first, but which you will grow to know and love (well maybe not love—but know, certainly). We could call it formal/academic/professional writing—or simply "House Style for Writing Class." To use the analogy of a business model, since many of you are (or will be) professionals in your respective fields, if you work in a context where writing is part of the job, your employer will often have a certain style of writing, or "house style," which the company considers appropriate for professional communication. It includes format (the way documents look) but goes beyond that to encompass ways of expressing ideas. In some work contexts, you may not even have to think too much about this style of expression because documents such as form letters (like the ones we receive from banks and credit card companies) already exist, and all you have to do is insert names and details according to the situation.

Someday, of course, when you get to be the one in charge, you can change the rules, come up with a whole new "form," and so on. Picasso did it in the art world; Glen Gould did it in music, and someday you may do it in your own field. For now, though, you need to show that you understand the basics: draw a picture with perspective, play a few scales (OK, not literally!)

To simplify my expectations of the basic requirements for writing, we have a "house style" in mind for our course. Not too surprisingly, it accords with the same general guidelines that would apply to any similar academic writing situation. However, as you may already know, even in academia, the "House Style" is not the same across the disciplines: a major divide is between the sciences (including the social sciences) and the arts (sometimes called "humanities"). In terms of format, that is, how documents look, you may already know that MLA (Modern Language Association) style differs significantly from that of the APA (American Psychological Association), and that MLA is popular in, for example, English classes!

Yet we also see subtler stylistic differences: for instance, passive voice as preferable in the "sciences," active voice in the "arts." In an English composition, for instance, we usually want to clarify and emphasize who does what: "This author uses analogy in his writing" (instead of saying "Analogy is used . . ."); in a biology lab report, though, we don't need (or want) to know that "Johnny heated the solution to 34°C"—we simply require the information that "the solution was heated to 34°C," as I'm sure any science professor would agree.

So, that's the first commandment: Heat the solution to 34°C. Kidding! Just checking to see if you're still awake. Actually, our first commandment of style for 1100 is to use active voice. Here's another example:

ACTIVE: Deborah kicked the dog.

PASSIVE: The dog was kicked (by Deborah).

OK, so in the active voice, the key aspect to notice is that the subject (Deborah) does the action (of kicking the dog). In the passive voice, the (poor) dog does not actually do anything, but is merely the (unfortunate) recipient of the action. Grammatically, note that the passive voice includes a form of the verb "to be" (the word "was" in this case) and the past participle of a verb ("kicked" in this case). Note also that the sentence in the passive voice would be grammatically correct and complete ("The dog was kicked") even if we left out the information of who did it ("by Deborah"). Hence the bank can tell you that your loan documents "have been misplaced" without telling you who misplaced them, and without taking the responsibility that would be implicit in the statement "we misplaced . . ."—let alone by naming a particular person.

In our own writing, then, to be clear, we will obey the FIRST COMMANDMENT of style and USE ACTIVE VOICE.

Indeed, several of our commandments for house style relate strongly to the concept of clarity. Since the opposite of clear is vague, at the level of word choice, we want to stay away from vague words. The one that some professors find the most annoying (and thus a no-brainer to avoid) is the word "thing." While useful in casual conversation, "things" have no real place in academic writing (nor in the professional word, for that matter). For instance, rather than saying that Peter Elbow advocates freewriting as one of the best "things" to do to get past a mental block, we could say, "freewriting is one of the best ways . . ." and so on. Notice how easily we can find a substitute for "thing"! This vague word has many friends of similar ilk, all too vague and tedious to list here, but use your best judgment and avoid vagueness scrupulously . . .

So, BE PRECISE: that's our SECOND COMMANDMENT.

Just as being precise means saying exactly what we mean, being concise means saying only what we mean—without extra words or phrases cluttering up the writing. So-called "weak expletive" constructions add words without adding meaning. Consider the sentence, "There is a dog on the lawn." What's the subject of the sentence? ("Dog.") What necessary information is in the word "there"? (None.) So, what should the sentence be? Right! "A dog is on the lawn." See how much shorter and clearer that sentence is? And so simple, a child could do it! And so can you. Rather than saying, "There is a scientific focus in this essay," we could say, "This essay has a scientific focus."

A simple formula for success: THIRD COMMANDMENT: BE CONCISE.

Of course, conciseness not only applies to the way we say what we say, but to the actual content itself. In an analytical essay, for instance, we definitely do not need the document to be self-referential; that is, we do not need to make any statements whatsoever about the essay we are writing. All of our statements should actually be about the topic, that is, the works (i.e., essays) we are discussing. We need to avoid self-referential wording, which is inherently redundant and is usually the result of an unclear thesis or a lack of a logical transition between ideas. Phrasing such as "in this essay," "the following paragraphs," and "as previously mentioned" are common examples of what not to do in this regard. On the subject of transitions, note that transitions of chronology, such as "first," "second," and "finally," are often self-referential to the essay, and thus are a weak way of connecting ideas: in other words, the points are in a certain order (first, second, etc.), only because you chose to put them in that order in your essay—not due to any inherent chronological order such as historical sequence. (Note how flagrantly we have disregarded this advice in putting together these ten guidelines—but that's professorial privilege—or perhaps poetic license!) In your essay, then, the basic idea will be to talk about the topic rather than the essay itself. While some documents (such as the one you are reading right now) can be appropriately self-referential, an analytical essay is not one of them. Instead of saying, "This paper will analyze the author's article and its use of various rhetorical strategies to connect with the audience," we could simply say, "This article uses various rhetorical strategies . . ."

FOURTH COMMANDMENT: (as they say in the Nike ads) JUST DO IT!

Hand in hand with being clearly on-topic goes specificity. If, for instance, you have the habit of using the word "this" to refer to a previous idea or concept in a general sort of way, you are not being specific enough in your choice of words. Fortunately, the solution is an easy one: simply make a habit of always adding a noun after the word "this" to ensure adequate specificity. Ask yourself, "this what?"—and stick in the appropriate word accordingly. If no clear answer comes to mind when you ask the question, you'll know that your thoughts—not just your words—are not sufficiently specific.

FIFTH COMMANDMENT: BE SPECIFIC.

One area in which specificity can unwittingly go to the dogs (you see how these commandments favor the dog motif) is in the vague use of the pronoun "it." This advice is not to discourage you from using "it" (a highly useful little word) altogether, of course—only to ensure that "it" always refers clearly to a previous noun, known as its "antecedent." Here's an appropriate use of "it": "This article is persuasive. It presents several examples in support of the argument." ("It" refers clearly to the antecedent, "article.") Consider, in contrast, this vague use of "it" (and by the way, this situation is a variant of the "weak expletive" construction): "It is clear in this essay that the author has a persuasive aim." (Note that "it" does not refer to any particular antecedent noun at all.)

Our SIXTH COMMANDMENT is thus to CHECK FOR CLEAR ANTECEDENTS (sounds a little indecent—but great advice nonetheless).

While we are on the subject of pronouns, we can also consider the advisability of being appropriately formal in academic writing. Actually, clarity and formality are both at work here. One of the most frequent questions students ask me about essay writing is whether or not to use the first person singular pronoun, "I." For a general composition course such as Writing 1100, some profs may give the advice to use "I" to talk about personal experience (e.g., "When I was traveling in Quebec last year, I observed . . ."), but not opinion (e.g., avoid phrasing such as "I think," "I feel," "in my opinion," "in my view"). When analyzing authors' essays, however, the advice is actually simpler: do not use "I." We need not think of this prohibition as removing ourselves from our personal response to the works in question; instead, we can think about shared experience with other readers. By the way, using "we" to include yourself among a general readership is quite acceptable. "My experiences give me insight into that author's article" would thus be better as "Those who have given considerable thought to their relevant experiences will have particular insight into this article," or, "we may draw upon personal experience for insight . . ." and so on.

And what about the second-person pronoun, "you"? Again, context is everything. The use of "you" can be appropriate if speaking directly to the person (or persons) reading the document, as we are doing right now; however, such an approach is not part of the conventions of literary analysis, as with the avoidance of "I," because instead of discussing individual reader responses, we assume the more general response of "the reader" or "readers." Hence, rather than saying, "As a twenty-first century North American, you may feel distant from Orwell's essay, which was written in mid-twentieth century Britain," we could say that "twenty-first century North American readers may feel distant . . ." and so on.

Hence our SEVENTH COMMANDMENT: USE APPROPRIATE PRONOUNS.

Much of this discussion thus touches on the appropriateness of what we say in an essay about literature: we remove individual/personal statements in favor of a more subjective, analytical approach. Personal judgments, or value judgments, are not appropriate for this type of essay. Calling an essay—or its author—"interesting," "brilliant," or some other term of praise, does not convey much in terms of meaning, except approval, even (or perhaps especially) if we're talking about an author whom most people would consider to be interesting and brilliant. And let's face reality: that author does not need your approval! Do not confuse your task here with that of a reviewer such as a columnist in a newspaper or magazine, whose job is to give a thumbs-up (or down) to a new book or film. As a student, your focus is on figuring out how the author does what he or she is doing—not judging how well he or she does it. So, judge not (now doesn't that sound biblical?)

The EIGHTH COMMANDMENT is to BE ANALYTICAL.

Just as considerations of appropriate content govern our choice of words (or "diction") in academic writing, so do considerations of formality. On the whole, our diction should be formal. Words such as "kid" (to mean "child"), "a lot" (to mean "considerably"), and "big" (to mean "significant") are fine for casual conversation, but not for an English essay. Don't go to the opposite extreme, however: "pretentious diction" is the result of trying to sound too educated, elegant, and sophisticated. Use your best judgment to choose the best words for the job. We need to keep in mind that the notion of formality is so important in academic writing that it sometimes trumps all else. We could certainly use the letter "R" to represent the word "are" (as is common practice in text messaging), but no one (one would hope) would do so in an academic essay. The same basic principle governs the avoidance of contractions and abbreviations in academic prose. Contracted forms such as "won't," "can't," and "aren't" are easy to replace with "will not," "cannot," and "are not," respectively. (Using possessive forms—as long as you do it properly—is fine). Similarly, we can use "such as" to preface an incomplete list, rather than sticking "and so on" at the end of it; we can write out "and" rather than using an ampersand ("&").

Put simply, to USE FORMAL DICTION is our NINTH COMMANDMENT.

The use of appropriate diction will make your document more appealing to an academic audience; you can also achieve that sense of appeal by making sure that everything you say flows together smoothly. We've already talked about transitions to some extent, but equally important aspects of that smooth flow (or "coherence") are using appropriate verb tenses (we use present for literary analysis—imagine that what's happening in the literary work is happening as you encounter it) and fitting quotations logically into your sentence structure. The good news is that you as a writer can actually alter the quoted material to fit into the sentence, using square brackets. The basic principle here is that the sentence should make perfect sense with the quoted material in it. (By the way, never refer to "the quote," and so on, per se; we want to avoid being self-referential in the essay).

TENTH COMMANDMENT: BE COHERENT.

And in conclusion, until these guidelines become so familiar that they're an unconscious part of the way you write an essay (as they are for me!), you might want to print them out and have them at your side as you prepare to do some academic writing. The word "commandment" is a joke, of course. No one is going to wag a finger at you (literally or metaphorically) and say "thou shalt not . . ." You won't fail, if you fail to observe these suggestions; nonetheless, they are important—so much so, that failure to observe even one of them could keep you from attaining your (undoubted) potential as a writer.

Someday, you may even be grateful! In a very real sense, all writers owe a debt to other writers, as this list is much indebted to George Orwell and others. Orwell, as you will discover (if you haven't already read his essay) gives his own set of guidelines (some of which we've echoed and modified here), then cheerfully announces that ultimately we all need to use our own judgment as writers—and that he has shamelessly violated all of his own rules (as we have done here, too!) The fact remains that rules are useful for discipline and training, in order to unleash your potential. Training? Leash? Whoa! Sounds like we're getting back to the dog metaphor again. Look, just follow the "house style" for our class, and the writing process will be a walk in the park.

Now, let's try practicing your proofreading skills. Check draft writing for the following:

 i. "This" → always add a noun after "this" for clarity

 ii. Pronouns → always make sure each pronoun has a clear antecedent (noun it replaces)

  - It (third person singular): note possessive form "its"

  - He/she; him/her; his/hers (third person singular; note we should strive for gender-neutral language)

  - They, them, their (third person plural)

  - You (second person singular or plural; uncommon in academic essays)

  - I (first person singular; uncommon in academic essays other than personal essays; avoid first-person statements of opinion)

  - We (first person plural; fine for academic writing as long as who "we" are is clear in context)

 iii. Vague quantifiers → big, a lot, and so on.

 iv. Idiom → be careful with overly used expressions, metaphors, and so on.

 v. Vague nouns, for example, "thing" → find a more specific and accurate word!

Next, consider the following examples, and find others in your own or a partner's writing:

A. Passive voice (in which the subject of the sentence receives rather than does the action)

PASSIVE: The dog was kicked by Deborah.

→ CHANGE TO ACTIVE: Deborah kicked the dog.

Further, for example,

_____

_____

B. Weak expletives with "there" + to be (in which "there" masquerades as the subject)

WEAK EXPLETIVE: There is a cat on the lawn.

→ DELETE "THERE": A cat is on the lawn.

Further, for example,

_____

_____

C. Weak expletives with "it" + to be

WEAK EXPLETIVE: It is important to study.

→ FIND THE REAL SUBJECT OF THE SENTENCE: Studying is important.

Further, for example,

_____

_____

D. Redundancy

REDUNDANT: My father is a man who is verbose and likes to talk too much.

→ DELETE REDUNDANT PHRASING: My father is verbose.

Further, for example,

_____

_____

E. Wordiness

WORDY: We need to make contact with them before any more time passes by.

→ USE CONCISE PHRASING: We need to contact them immediately.

Further, for example,

_____

_____

Now, try to edit the following sentences. The type of stylistic issue that the sentence suffers from is indicated for you; your task is to rewrite the sentence in such a way as to solve the problem without changing the meaning or making any grammatical errors. Try reading the new sentence, as you have revised it, out loud to see if it sounds clear and coherent.

1. Weak expletive construction (change the phrasing to avoid "there"):

    There are several causes of the problems with drug abuse in contemporary Canadian society.

    _____

    _____

2. Vague use of the pronoun "it" (use a clear subject for the sentence):

    It is important to understand that social media could ultimately destroy what we most value about human communication.

    _____

    _____

3. Unclear reference to "this" (always add a noun directly after "this" for clarity):

    If we value our identity as Canadians, we will always be aware of what this means.

    _____

    _____

4. Informal use of second-person pronoun (do not use "you" in formal writing):

    When you are lonely, the best strategy is to somehow reach out to the people around you who care about your situation.

    _____

    _____

5. Use of first-person singular to introduce an argument (state the point directly without using "I"):

    Like many other people of my generation, I believe that ownership of property can actually be a positive moral force, and in my view, the popularity of real estate in Vancouver and other major urban centers reflects this trend, in my opinion.

    _____

    _____

6. Use of contractions (write out full forms without apostrophes):

Society can't afford to ignore the issue of poverty, no matter whom it's affecting; it'll affect everyone in some way if we don't take action against it.

_____

_____

7. Self-referential statements regarding a document (do not refer to the writing process itself):

In this essay, I will demonstrate in the following paragraphs the need for greater attention to Native issues in Canada; as previously mentioned above, contemporary activists see a need for education, autonomy, and equality for aboriginal Canadians.

_____

_____

8. Slang, informal language, vague words, overly used expressions, and so on (reword as necessary):

To coin a phrase, the big thing about a lot of scientific discoveries is that they come at a humongous cost.

_____

_____

9. Passive voice (change to active, in which the subject performs the action of the verb):

Essays that are written by students are often quite different from those that are produced by professional authors.

_____

_____

10. Dangling and misplaced modifiers (put the elements of the sentence in a logical order):

As an officer representing the authority in an autobiographical essay of the British government in a colonial nation, an elephant being shot to death is a powerful symbol of the need for change.

_____

_____

Spelling Checks and Grammar Checks

Your word processing program may help you with spelling and grammar checks when you are writing an essay at home. These automatic checks are far from foolproof however, as evidenced by a student essay I once read, entitled "The Unemployment Rat in Canada" (they meant "Rate") or my friend's memory of submitting an essay called "The Pheasant Revolt" (should have been "Peasant")! Read back over what you have written—as difficult as it may be to force yourself to do it!! Keep in mind that these technical aspects of writing are part of the broader context of feedback and evaluation. Note the following assessment categories:

Able to Write and Edit Independently

This category represents our goal for the course: to have a clear and coherent writing style, with few—if any—grammatical errors; to introduce, develop, and conclude a discussion effectively; to create a bond of interest and respect with the reader. Writers who begin the course at this level can work on fine-tuning their skills in order to produce more lucid and appealing prose, suited to academic and professional communications.

Able to Write and Edit with Moderate Support

Given sufficient time and an adequate focus, many students can achieve a reasonable standard of writing; the goal is to become one's own best editor instead of relying on someone else (i.e., the instructor) to spot and/or correct any issues requiring revision. In an English course, expression is as important as content, so even those who have great ideas (i.e., a strong argument) and effective development may need to work on shaping their prose style.

Able to Write and Edit with Guided Support

Significant work may be necessary in order to bring the writing in this category up to postsecondary standards. A comprehensive review of basic grammar is a prerequisite for more sophisticated refinements, as many of the sentences in the composition may contain grammatical errors. During the semester, students may be able to make sufficient progress by doing extra work on their editing skills.

Able to Write and Edit with Direct Support

At this point, writing requires extensive editing in order to be understood by the reader. It may be necessary in the short term to simplify the sentence structure and vocabulary, prior to developing a more advanced approach. Analogously, shorter compositions to be edited in greater detail will be more useful than lengthy documents in which frequent and serious errors in language obscure the intended meaning. Those who are writing in English as an Additional Language will find that the task poses many challenges, especially when the ideas are complex—but the results will ultimately be more than worth it!

Finding and Correcting Glitches

A glitch is a careless or unintentional error that is usually the result of a lack of attention to detail, as sometimes happens when we are writing under pressure (e.g., in class), such as an in-class essay, midterm, or final exam.

Strategies for Writing an Essay in Class

Timing Tip: tell yourself you have at least twenty minutes less than you actually do (thus leaving adequate time for editing and proofreading)

PREWRITING
Five to ten minutes

Try freewriting, brainstorming, mind mapping, questioning, or any other technique

PLANNING
Five to ten minutes

Title: assignment name plus your own original title

Introduction: "hook" to capture the reader's interest; thesis

Body: paragraph topics × 2–3

Conclusion: consequences/implications

DRAFTING
Double-space, write legibly; indent each paragraph

EDITING
Read through from beginning to end to ensure unity and coherence, then start with the final sentence, second-last sentence, and so on, going in reverse order through the document back to the beginning.

Consider your personal checklist of potential problem areas/errors you tend to make, and so on.

Feel confident that you are submitting your best work!

"After all, I am not so violently bent upon my own opinion, as to reject any offer, proposed by wise men, which shall be found equally innocent, cheap, easy, and effectual."

—*Jonathan Swift, "A Modest Proposal"*

Review Exercise: Peer Editing

Your instructor will provide some sample essay prompts from past final exams in class. Step one is to plan, write, and edit the essay within the given time limit; step two is to show your work to a partner and participate in a peer editing workshop in which you provide critical commentary on each other's work, in light of the editing advice we have covered. Have fun!

SECTION 7
READINGS

Fables

Aesop

The Lion and the Mouse

Once when a Lion was asleep, a little Mouse began running up and down upon him; this soon wakened the Lion, who placed his huge paw upon him, and opened his big jaws to swallow him. "Pardon, O King," cried the little Mouse: "forgive me this time, I shall never forget it: who knows but what I may be able to do you a turn some of these days?" The Lion was so tickled at the idea of the Mouse being able to help him that he lifted up his paw and let him go. Sometime after the Lion was caught in a trap, and the hunters who desired to carry him alive to the King, tied him to a tree while they went in search of a wagon to carry him on. Just then the little Mouse happened to pass by, and seeing the sad plight in which the Lion was, went up to him and soon gnawed away the ropes that bound the King of the Beasts. "Was I not right?" said the little Mouse.

Little friends may prove great friends.

The Wolf in Sheep's Clothing

A Wolf found great difficulty in getting at the sheep owing to the vigilance of the shepherd and his dogs. But one day it found the skin of a sheep that had been flayed and thrown aside, so it put it on over its own pelt and strolled down among the sheep. The Lamb that belonged to the sheep, whose skin the Wolf was wearing, began to follow the Wolf in the Sheep's clothing; so, leading the Lamb a little apart, he soon made a meal off her, and for some time he succeeded in deceiving the sheep, and enjoying hearty meals.

Appearances are deceptive.

The Goose with the Golden Eggs

One day a countryman going to the nest of his Goose found there an egg all yellow and glittering. When he took it up, it was as heavy as lead and he was going to throw it away, because he thought a trick had been played upon him. But he took it home on second thoughts, and soon found to his delight that it was an egg of pure gold. Every morning the same thing occurred, and he soon became rich by selling his eggs. As he grew rich, he grew greedy; and thinking to get at once all the gold the Goose could give, he killed it and opened it only to find nothing.

Greed oft o'er reaches itself.

The Hare and the Tortoise

The Hare was once boasting of his speed before the other animals. "I have never yet been beaten," said he, "when I put forth my full speed. I challenge any one here to race with me."

The Tortoise said quietly, "I accept your challenge."

"That is a good joke," said the Hare; "I could dance round you all the way."

"Keep your boasting till you've beaten," answered the Tortoise. "Shall we race?"

So a course was fixed and a start was made. The Hare darted almost out of sight at once, but soon stopped and, to show his contempt for the Tortoise, lay down to have a nap. The Tortoise plodded on and plodded on, and when the Hare awoke from his nap, he saw the Tortoise just near the winning post and could not run up in time to save the race. Then said the Tortoise:

"Plodding wins the race."

The Town Mouse and the Country Mouse

Now you must know that a Town Mouse once upon a time went on a visit to his cousin in the country. He was rough and ready, this cousin, but he loved his town friend and made him heartily welcome. Beans and bacon, cheese and bread, were all he had to offer, but he offered them freely. The Town Mouse rather turned up his long nose at this country fare, and said: "I cannot understand, Cousin, how you can put up with such poor food as this, but of course you cannot expect anything better in the country; come with me and I will show you how to live. When you have been in town a week you will wonder how you could ever have stood a country life." No sooner said than done: the two mice set off for the town and arrived at the Town Mouse's residence late at night. "You will want some refreshment after our long journey," said the polite Town Mouse, and took his friend into the grand dining room. There they found the remains of a fine feast, and soon the two mice were eating up jellies and cakes and all that was nice. Suddenly they heard growling and barking. "What is that?" said the Country Mouse. "It is only the dogs of the house," answered the other. "Only!" said the Country Mouse. "I do not like that music at my dinner." Just at that moment, the door flew open, in came two huge mastiffs, and the two mice had to scamper down and run off. "Good-bye, Cousin," said the Country Mouse, "What! going so soon?" said the other. "Yes," he replied;

"Better beans and bacon in peace than cakes and ale in fear."

The Fox and the Crow

A Fox once saw a Crow fly off with a piece of cheese in its beak and settle on a branch of a tree. "That's for me, as I am a Fox," said Master Reynard, and he walked up to the foot of the tree. "Good-day, Mistress Crow," he cried. "How well you are looking to-day: how glossy your feathers; how bright your eye. I feel sure your voice must surpass that of other birds, just as your figure does; let me hear but one song from you that I may greet you as the Queen of Birds." The Crow lifted up her head and began to caw her best, but the moment she opened her mouth, the piece of cheese fell to the ground, only to be snapped up by Master Fox. "That will do," said he. "That was all I wanted. In exchange for your cheese I will give you a piece of advice for the future." "Do not trust flatterers."

On Education Politics: Book Eight
Aristotle (translated by Benjamin Jowett)

I

NO ONE will doubt that the legislator should direct his attention above all to the education of youth; for the neglect of education does harm to the constitution. The citizen should be molded to suit the form of government under which he lives. For each government has a peculiar character which originally formed and which continues to preserve it. The character of democracy creates democracy, and the character of oligarchy creates oligarchy; and always the better the character, the better the government.

Again, for the exercise of any faculty or art a previous training and habituation are required; clearly therefore for the practice of virtue. And since the whole city has one end, it is manifest that education should be one and the same for all, and that it should be public, and not private—not as at present, when everyone looks after his own children separately, and gives them separate instruction of the sort which he thinks best; the training in things which are of common interest should be the same for all. Neither must we suppose that any one of the citizens belongs to himself, for they all belong to the state, and are each of them a part of the state, and the care of each part is inseparable from the care of the whole. In this particular as in some others the Lacedaemonians are to be praised, for they take the greatest pains about their children, and make education the business of the state.

II

That education should be regulated by law and should be an affair of state is not to be denied, but what should be the character of this public education, and how young persons should be educated, are questions which remain to be considered. As things are, there is disagreement about the subjects. For mankind are by no means agreed about the things to be taught, whether we look to virtue or the best life. Neither is it clear whether education is more concerned with intellectual or with moral virtue. The existing practice is perplexing; no one knows on what principle we should proceed—should the useful in life, or should virtue, or should the higher knowledge, be the aim of our training; all three opinions have been entertained. Again, about the means, there is no agreement; for different persons, starting with different ideas about the nature of virtue, naturally disagree about the practice of it. There can be no doubt that children should be taught those useful things which are really necessary, but not all useful things; for occupations are divided into liberal and illiberal; and to young children should be imparted only such kinds of knowledge as will be useful to them without vulgarizing them. And any occupation, art, or science, which makes the body or soul or mind of the freeman less fit for the practice or exercise of virtue, is vulgar; wherefore we call those arts vulgar which tend to deform the body, and likewise all paid employments, for they absorb and degrade the mind. There are also some liberal arts quite proper for a freeman to acquire, but only in a certain degree, and if he attend to them too closely, in order to attain perfection in them, the same evil effects will follow. The object also which a man sets before him makes a great difference; if he does or learns anything for his own sake or for the sake of his friends, or with a view to excellence the action will not appear illiberal; but if done for the sake of others, the very same action will be thought menial and servile. The received subjects of instruction, as I have already remarked, are partly of a liberal and party of an illiberal character.

III

The customary branches of education are in number four; they are—(1) reading and writing, (2) gymnastic exercises, (3) music, to which is sometimes added, (4) drawing. Of these, reading and writing and drawing are regarded as useful for the purposes of life in a variety of ways, and gymnastic exercises are thought to infuse courage. Concerning music, a doubt may be raised—in our own day, most men cultivate it for the sake of pleasure, but originally it was included in education, because nature herself, as has been often said, requires that we should be able, not only to work well, but to use leisure well; for, as I must repeat once again, the first principle of all action is leisure. Both are required, but leisure is better than occupation and is its end; and therefore the question must be asked, what ought we to do when at leisure? Clearly we ought not to be amusing ourselves, for then amusement would be the end of life. But if this is inconceivable, and amusement is needed more amid serious occupations than at other times (for he who is hard at work has need of relaxation, and amusement gives relaxation, whereas occupation is always accompanied with exertion and effort), we should introduce amusements only at suitable times, and they should be our medicines, for the emotion which they create in the soul is a relaxation, and from the pleasure we obtain rest. But leisure of itself gives pleasure and happiness and enjoyment of life, which are experienced, not by the busy man, but by those who have leisure. For he who is occupied has in view some end which he has not attained; but happiness is an end, since all men deem it to be accompanied with pleasure and not with pain. This pleasure, however, is regarded differently by different persons, and varies according to the habit of individuals; the pleasure of the best man is the best, and springs from the noblest sources. It is clear then that there are branches of learning and education which we must study merely with a view to leisure spent in intellectual activity, and these are to be valued for their own sake; whereas those kinds of knowledge which are useful in business are to be deemed necessary, and exist for the sake of other things. And therefore our fathers admitted music into education, not on the ground either of its necessity or utility, for it is not necessary, nor indeed useful in the same manner as reading and writing, which are useful in moneymaking, in the management of a household, in the acquisition of knowledge, and in political life, nor like drawing, useful for a more correct judgment of the works of artists, nor again like gymnastic, which gives health and strength; for neither of these is to be gained from music. There remains, then, the use of music for intellectual enjoyment in leisure; which is in fact evidently the reason of its introduction, this being one of the ways in which it is thought that a freeman should pass his leisure; as Homer says,

"But he who alone should be called to the pleasant feast," and afterward he speaks of others whom he describes as inviting

"The bard who would delight them all."

And in another place, Odysseus says there is no better way of passing life than when men's hearts are merry and the

"banqueters in the hall, sitting in order, hear the voice of the minstrel."

It is evident, then, that there is a sort of education in which parents should train their sons, not as being useful or necessary, but because it is liberal or noble. Whether this is of one kind only, or of more than one, and if so, what they are, and how they are to be imparted, must hereafter be determined. Thus much we are now in a position to say, that the ancients witness to us; for their opinion may be gathered from the fact that music is one of the received and traditional branches of education. Further, it is clear that children should be instructed in some useful things—for example, in reading and writing—not only for their usefulness, but also because many other sorts of knowledge are acquired through them. With a like view they may be taught drawing, not to prevent their making mistakes in their own purchases, or in order that they may not be imposed upon in the buying or selling of articles, but perhaps rather because it makes them judges of the beauty of the human form. To be always seeking after the useful does not become free and exalted souls. Now it is clear that in education practice must be used before theory, and the body be trained before the mind; and therefore boys should be handed over to the trainer, who creates in them the roper habit of body, and to the wrestling master, who teaches them their exercises.

IV

Of those states which in our own day seem to take the greatest care of children, some aim at producing in them an athletic habit, but they only injure their forms and stunt their growth. Although the Lacedaemonians have not fallen into this mistake, yet they brutalize their children by laborious exercises which they think will make them courageous. But in truth, as we have often repeated, education should not be exclusively, or principally, directed to this end. And even if we suppose the Lacedaemonians to be right in their end, they do not attain it. For among barbarians and among animals courage is found associated, not with the greatest ferocity, but with a gentle and lion like temper. There are many races who are ready enough to kill and eat men, such as the Achaeans and Heniochi, who both live about the Black Sea; and there are other mainland tribes, as bad or worse, who all live by plunder, but have no courage. It is notorious that the Lacedaemonians themselves, while they alone were assiduous in their laborious drill, were superior to others, but now they are beaten both in war and gymnastic exercises. For their ancient superiority did not depend on their mode of training their youth, but only on the circumstance that they trained them when their only rivals did not. Hence we may infer that what is noble, not what is brutal, should have the first place; no wolf or other wild animal will face a really noble danger; such dangers are for the brave man. And parents who devote their children to gymnastics while they neglect their necessary education, in reality vulgarize them; for they make them useful to the art of statesmanship in one quality only, and even in this the argument proves them to be inferior to others. We should judge the Lacedaemonians not from what they have been, but from what they are; for now they have rivals who compete with their education; formerly they had none.

It is an admitted principle, that gymnastic exercises should be employed in education, and that for children they should be of a lighter kind, avoiding severe diet or painful toil, lest the growth of the body be impaired. The evil of excessive training in early years is strikingly proved by the example of the Olympic victors; for not more than two or three of them have gained a prize both as boys and as men; their early training and severe gymnastic exercises exhausted their constitutions. When boyhood is over, three years should be spent in other studies; the period of life which follows may then be devoted to hard exercise and strict diet. Men ought not to labor at the same time with their minds and with their bodies; for the two kinds of labor are opposed to one another; the labor of the mind impedes the body.

V

Concerning music there are some questions which we have already raised; these we may now resume and carry further; and our remarks will serve as a prelude to this or any other discussion of the subject. It is not easy to determine the nature of music, or why anyone should have a knowledge of it. Shall we say, for the sake of amusement and relaxation, like sleep or drinking, which are not good in themselves, but are pleasant, and at the same time "care to cease," as Euripides says? And for this end men also appoint music, and make use of all three alike—sleep, drinking, music—to which some add dancing. Or shall we argue that music conduces to virtue, on the ground that it can form our minds and habituate us to true pleasures as our bodies are made by gymnastic to be of a certain character? Or shall we say that it contributes to the enjoyment of leisure and mental cultivation, which is a third alternative? Now obviously youths are not to be instructed with a view to their amusement, for learning is no amusement, but is accompanied with pain. Neither is intellectual enjoyment suitable to boys of that age, for it is the end, and that which is imperfect cannot attain the perfect or end. But perhaps it may be said that boys learn music for the sake of the amusement which they will have when they are grown up. If so, why should they learn themselves, and not, like the Persian and Median kings, enjoy the pleasure and instruction which is derived from hearing others? (For surely persons who have made music the business and profession of their lives will be better performers than those who practice only long enough to learn). If they must learn music, on the same principle they should learn cookery, which is absurd. And even granting that music may form the character, the objection still holds: why should we learn ourselves? Why cannot we attain true pleasure and form a correct judgment from hearing others, like the Lacedaemonians?—for they, without learning music, nevertheless can correctly judge, as they say, of good and bad melodies. Or again, if music should be used to promote cheerfulness and refined intellectual enjoyment, the objection still remains—why should we learn ourselves instead of enjoying the performances of others? We may illustrate what we are saying by our conception of the Gods; for in the poets Zeus does not himself sing or play on the lyre. Nay, we call professional performers vulgar; no freeman would play or sing unless he were intoxicated or in jest. But these matters may be left for the present.

The first question is whether music is or is not to be a part of education. Of the three things mentioned in our discussion, which does it produce?—education or amusement or intellectual enjoyment, for it may be reckoned under all three, and seems to share in the nature of all of them. Amusement is for the sake of relaxation, and relaxation is of necessity sweet, for it is the remedy of pain caused by toil; and intellectual enjoyment is universally acknowledged to contain an element not only of the noble but of the pleasant, for happiness is made up of both. All men agree that music is one of the pleasantest things, whether with or without songs; as Musaeus says:

"Song to mortals of all things the sweetest."

Hence and with good reason it is introduced into social gatherings and entertainments, because it makes the hearts of men glad: so that on this ground alone we may assume that the young ought to be trained in it. For innocent pleasures are not only in harmony with the perfect end of life, but they also provide relaxation. And whereas men rarely attain the end, but often rest by the way and amuse themselves, not only with a view to a further end, but also for the pleasure's sake, it may be well at times to let them find a refreshment in music. It sometimes happens that men make amusement the end, for the end probably contains some element of pleasure, though not any ordinary or lower pleasure; but they mistake the lower for the higher, and in seeking for the one find the other, since every pleasure has a likeness to the end of action. For the end is not eligible for the sake of any future good, nor do the pleasures which we have described exist for the sake of any future good but of the past, that is to say, they are the alleviation of past toils and pains. And we may infer this to be the reason why men seek happiness from these pleasures.

But music is pursued, not only as an alleviation of past toil, but also as providing recreation. And who can say whether, having this use, it may not also have a nobler one? In addition to this common pleasure, felt and shared in by all (for the pleasure given by music is natural, and therefore adapted to all ages and characters), may it not have also some influence over the character and the soul? It must have such an influence if characters are affected by it. And that they are so affected is proved in many ways, and not least by the power which the songs of Olympus exercise; for beyond question they inspire enthusiasm, and enthusiasm is an emotion of the ethical part of the soul. Besides, when men hear imitations, even apart from the rhythms and tunes themselves, their feelings move in sympathy. Since then music is a pleasure, and virtue consists in rejoicing and loving and hating aright, there is clearly nothing which we are so much concerned to acquire and to cultivate as the power of forming right judgments, and of taking delight in good dispositions and noble actions. Rhythm and melody supply imitations of anger and gentleness, and also of courage and temperance, and of all the qualities contrary to these, and of the other qualities of character, which hardly fall short of the actual affections, as we know from our own experience, for in listening to such strains our souls undergo a change. The habit of feeling pleasure or pain at mere representations is not far removed from the same feeling about realities; for example, if any one delights in the sight of a statue for its beauty only, it necessarily follows that the sight of the original will be pleasant to him. The objects of no other sense, such as taste or touch, have any resemblance to moral qualities; in visible objects there is only a little, for there are figures which are of a moral character, but only to a slight extent, and all do not participate in the feeling about them. Again, figures and colors are not imitations, but signs, of moral habits, indications which the body gives of states of feeling. The connection of them with morals is slight, but in so far as there is any, young men should be taught to look, not at the works of Pauson, but at those of Polygnotus, or any other painter or sculptor who expresses moral ideas. On the other hand, even in mere melodies, there is an imitation of character, for the musical modes differ essentially from one another, and those who hear them are differently affected by each. Some of them make men sad and grave, like the so-called Mixolydian, others enfeeble the mind, like the relaxed modes, another, again, produces a moderate and settled temper, which appears to be the peculiar effect of the Dorian; the Phrygian inspires enthusiasm. The whole subject has been well treated by philosophical writers on this branch of education, and they confirm their arguments by facts. The same principles apply to rhythms; some have a character of rest, others of motion, and of these latter again, some have a more vulgar, others a nobler movement. Enough has been said to show that music has a power of forming the character, and should therefore be introduced into the education of the young. The study is suited to the stage of youth, for young persons will not, if they can help, endure anything which is not sweetened by pleasure, and music has a natural sweetness. There seems to be in us a sort of affinity to musical modes and rhythms, which makes some philosophers say that the soul is a tuning, others, that it possesses tuning.

VI

And now we have to determine the question which has been already raised, whether children should be themselves taught to sing and play or not. Clearly there is a considerable difference made in the character by the actual practice of the art. It is difficult, if not impossible, for those who do not perform to be good judges of the performance of others. Besides, children should have something to do, and the rattle of Archytas, which people give to their children in order to amuse them and prevent them from breaking anything in the house, was a capital invention, for a young thing cannot be quiet. The rattle is a toy suited to the infant mind, and education is a rattle or toy for children of a larger growth. We conclude then that they should be taught music in such a way as to become not only critics but performers.

The question what is or is not suitable for different ages may be easily answered; nor is there any difficulty in meeting the objection of those who say that the study of music is vulgar. We reply (1) in the first place, that they who are to be judges must also be performers, and that they should begin to practice early, although when they are older, they may be spared the execution; they must have learned to appreciate what is good and to delight in it, thanks to the knowledge which they acquired in their youth. As to (2) the vulgarizing effect which music is supposed to exercise, this is a question which we shall have no difficulty in determining, when we have considered to what extent freemen who are being trained to political virtue should pursue the art, what melodies and what rhythms they should be allowed to use, and what instruments should be employed in teaching them to play; for even the instrument makes a difference. The answer to the objection turns upon these distinctions; for it is quite possible that certain methods of teaching and learning music do really have a degrading effect. It is evident then that the learning of music ought not to impede the business of riper years, or to degrade the body or render it unfit for civil or military training, whether for bodily exercises at the time or for later studies.

The right measure will be attained if students of music stop short of the arts which are practiced in professional contests, and do not seek to acquire those fantastic marvels of execution which are now the fashion in such contests, and from these have passed into education. Let the young practice even such music as we have prescribed, only until they are able to feel delight in noble melodies and rhythms, and not merely in that common part of music in which every slave or child and even some animals find pleasure.

From these principles, we may also infer what instruments should be used. The flute, or any other instrument which requires great skill, as, for example, the harp, ought not to be admitted into education, but only such as will make intelligent students of music or of the other parts of education. Besides, the flute is not an instrument which is expressive of moral character; it is too exciting. The proper time for using it is when the performance aims not at instruction, but at the relief of the passions. And there is a further objection; the impediment which the flute presents to the use of the voice detracts from its educational value. The ancients therefore were right in forbidding the flute to youths and freemen, although they had once allowed it. For when their wealth gave them a greater inclination to leisure, and they had loftier notions of excellence, being also elated with their success, both before and after the Persian War, with more zeal than discernment they pursued every kind of knowledge, and so they introduced the flute into education. At Lacedaemon, there was a choragus who led the chorus with a flute, and at Athens, the instrument became so popular that most freemen could play upon it. The popularity is shown by the tablet which Thrasippus dedicated when he furnished the chorus to Ecphantides. Later experience enabled men to judge what was or was not really conducive to virtue, and they rejected both the flute and several other old-fashioned instruments, such as the Lydian harp, the many-stringed lyre, the "heptagon," "triangle," "sambuca," the like—which are intended only to give pleasure to the hearer, and require extraordinary skill of hand. There is a meaning also in the myth of the ancients, which tells how Athene invented the flute and then threw it away. It was not a bad idea of theirs, that the Goddess disliked the instrument because it made the face ugly; but with still more reason may we say that she rejected it because the acquirement of flute playing contributes nothing to the mind, since to Athene we ascribe both knowledge and art.

Thus then we reject the professional instruments and also the professional mode of education in music (and by professional, we mean that which is adopted in contests), for in this the performer practices the art, not for the sake of his own improvement, but in order to give pleasure, and that of a vulgar sort, to his hearers. For this reason, the execution of such music is not the part of a freeman but of a paid performer, and the result is that the performers are vulgarized, for the end at which they aim is bad. The vulgarity of the spectator tends to lower the character of the music and therefore of the performers; they look to him—he makes them what they are, and fashions even their bodies by the movements which he expects them to exhibit.

VII

We have also to consider rhythms and modes, and their use in education. Shall we use them all or make a distinction? And shall the same distinction be made for those who practice music with a view to education, or shall it be some other? Now we see that music is produced by melody and rhythm, and we ought to know what influence these have respectively on education, and whether we should prefer excellence in melody or excellence in rhythm. But as the subject has been very well treated by many musicians of the present day, and also by philosophers who have had considerable experience of musical education, to these we would refer the more exact student of the subject; we shall only speak of it now after the manner of the legislator, stating the general principles.

We accept the division of melodies proposed by certain philosophers into ethical melodies, melodies of action, and passionate or inspiring melodies, each having, as they say, a mode corresponding to it. But we maintain further that music should be studied, not for the sake of one, but of many benefits, that is to say, with a view to (1) education, (2) purgation (the word "purgation" we use at present without explanation, but when hereafter we speak of poetry, we will treat the subject with more precision); music may also serve (3) for enjoyment, for relaxation, and for recreation after exertion. It is clear, therefore, that all the modes must be employed by us, but not all of them in the same manner. In education, the most ethical modes are to be preferred, but in listening to the performances of others, we may admit the modes of action and passion also. For feelings such as pity and fear, or, again, enthusiasm, exist very strongly in some souls, and have more or less influence over all. Some persons fall into a religious frenzy, whom we see as a result of the sacred melodies—when they have used the melodies that excite the soul to mystic frenzy—restored as though they had found healing and purgation. Those who are influenced by pity or fear, and every emotional nature, must have a like experience, and others in so far as each is susceptible to such emotions, and all are in a manner purged and their souls lightened and delighted. The purgative melodies likewise give an innocent pleasure to mankind. Such are the modes and the melodies in which those who perform music at the theater should be invited to compete. But since the spectators are of two kinds—the one free and educated, and the other a vulgar crowd composed of mechanics, laborers, and the like—there ought to be contests and exhibitions instituted for the relaxation of the second class also. And the music will correspond to their minds; for as their minds are perverted from the natural state, so there are perverted modes and highly strung and unnaturally colored melodies. A man receives pleasure from what is natural to him, and therefore professional musicians may be allowed to practice this lower sort of music before an audience of a lower type. But, for the purposes of education, as I have already said, those modes and melodies should be employed which are ethical, such as the Dorian, as we said before; though we may include any others which are approved by philosophers who have had a musical education. The Socrates of the Republic is wrong in retaining only the Phrygian mode along with the Dorian, and the more so because he rejects the flute; for the Phrygian is to the modes what the flute is to musical instruments—both of them are exciting and emotional. Poetry proves this, for Bacchic frenzy and all similar emotions are most suitably expressed by the flute, and are better set to the Phrygian than to any other mode. The dithyramb, for example, is acknowledged to be Phrygian, a fact of which the connoisseurs of music offer many proofs, saying, among other things, that Philoxenus, having attempted to compose his Mysians as a dithyramb in the Dorian mode, found it impossible, and fell back by the very nature of things into the more appropriate Phrygian. All men agree that the Dorian music is the gravest and manliest. And whereas we say that the extremes should be avoided and the mean followed, and whereas the Dorian is a mean between the other modes, it is evident that our youth should be taught the Dorian music.

Two principles have to be kept in view, what is possible, what is becoming: at these every man ought to aim. But even these are relative to age; the old, who have lost their powers, cannot very well sing the high-strung modes, and nature herself seems to suggest that their songs should be of the more relaxed kind. Wherefore the musicians likewise blame Socrates, and with justice, for rejecting the relaxed modes in education under the idea that they are intoxicating, not in the ordinary sense of intoxication (for wine rather tends to excite men), but because they have no strength in them. And so, with a view also to the time of life when men begin to grow old, they ought to practice the gentler modes and melodies as well as the others, and, further, any mode, such as the Lydian above all others appears to be, which is suited to children of tender age, and possesses the elements both of order and of education. Thus it is clear that education should be based upon three principles—the mean, the possible, the becoming, these three.

The Origin of Species by Means of Natural Selection (excerpted)

Charles Darwin

CHAPTER III

Struggle for Existence

Nothing is easier than to admit in words the truth of the universal struggle for life, or more difficult—at least I have found it so—than constantly to bear this conclusion in mind. Yet unless it be thoroughly engrained in the mind, the whole economy of nature, with every fact on distribution, rarity, abundance, extinction, and variation, will be dimly seen or quite misunderstood. We behold the face of nature bright with gladness, we often see superabundance of food; we do not see or we forget, that the birds which are idly singing round us mostly live on insects or seeds, and are thus constantly destroying life; or we forget how largely these songsters, and their eggs, and their nestlings, are destroyed by birds and beasts of prey; we do not always bear in mind, that, though food may be now superabundant, it is not so at all seasons of each recurring year.

* * *

A struggle for existence inevitably follows from the high rate at which all organic beings tend to increase. Every being, which during its natural lifetime produces several eggs or seeds, must suffer destruction during some period of its life, and during some season or occasional year, otherwise, on the principle of geometrical increase, its numbers would quickly become so inordinately great that no country could support the product. Hence, as more individuals are produced than can possibly survive, there must in every case be a struggle for existence, either one individual with another of the same species, or with the individuals of distinct species, or with the physical conditions of life. It is the doctrine of Malthus applied with manifold force to the whole animal and vegetable kingdoms; for in this case, there can be no artificial increase of food, and no prudential restraint from marriage. Although some species may be now increasing, more or less rapidly, in numbers, all cannot do so, for the world would not hold them.

There is no exception to the rule that every organic being naturally increases at so high a rate, that, if not destroyed, the earth would soon be covered by the progeny of a single pair. Even slow-breeding man has doubled in twenty-five years, and at this rate, in less than a thousand years, there would literally not be standing room for his progeny. Linnaeus has calculated that if an annual plant produced only two seeds—and there is no plant so unproductive as this—and their seedlings next year produced two, and so on, then in twenty years, there would be a million plants. The elephant is reckoned the slowest breeder of all known animals, and I have taken some pains to estimate its probable minimum rate

Source: From *The Origin of Species* by Charles Darwin, 1859.

of natural increase; it will be safest to assume that it begins breeding when thirty years old, and goes on breeding till ninety years old, bringing forth six young in the interval, and surviving till one hundred years old; if this be so, after a period of from 740 to 750 years, there would be nearly nineteen million elephants alive, descended from the first pair.

* * *

As the species of the same genus usually have, though by no means invariably, much similarity in habits and constitution, and always in structure, the struggle will generally be more severe between them, if they come into competition with each other, than between the species of distinct genera. We see this in the recent extension over parts of the United States of one species of swallow having caused the decrease of another species. The recent increase of the missel thrush in parts of Scotland has caused the decrease of the song thrush. How frequently we hear of one species of rat taking the place of another species under the most different climates! In Russia, the small Asiatic cockroach has everywhere driven before it its great congener. In Australia, the imported hive bee is rapidly exterminating the small, stingless native bee. One species of charlock has been known to supplant another species; and so in other cases. We can dimly see why the competition should be most severe between allied forms, which fill nearly the same place in the economy of nature; but probably in no one case could we precisely say why one species has been victorious over another in the great battle of life.

A corollary of the highest importance may be deduced from the foregoing remarks, namely, that the structure of every organic being is related, in the most essential yet often hidden manner, to that of all the other organic beings, with which it comes into competition for food or residence, or from which it has to escape, or on which it preys. This is obvious in the structure of the teeth and talons of the tiger; and in that of the legs and claws of the parasite which clings to the hair on the tiger's body. But in the beautifully plumed seed of the dandelion, and in the flattened and fringed legs of the water beetle, the relation seems at first confined to the elements of air and water. Yet the advantage of plumed seeds no doubt stands in the closest relation to the land being already thickly clothed with other plants; so that the seeds may be widely distributed and fall on unoccupied ground. In the water beetle, the structure of its legs, so well adapted for diving, allows it to compete with other aquatic insects, to hunt for its own prey, and to escape serving as prey to other animals.

CHAPTER IV

Natural Selection; or the Survival of the Fittest

How will the struggle for existence, briefly discussed in the last chapter, act in regard to variation? Can the principle of selection, which we have seen is so potent in the hands of man, apply under nature? I think we shall see that it can act most efficiently. Let the endless number of slight variations and individual differences occurring in our domestic productions, and, in a lesser degree, in those under nature, be borne in mind; as well as the strength of the hereditary tendency. . . . Let it also be borne in mind how infinitely complex and close fitting are the mutual relations of all organic beings to each other and to their physical conditions of life; and consequently what infinitely varied diversities of structure might be of use to each being under changing conditions of life. Can it, then, be thought improbable, seeing that variations useful to man have undoubtedly occurred, that other variations useful in some way to each being in the great and complex battle of life, should occur in the course of many successive generations? If such do occur, can we doubt (remembering that many more individuals are born than can possibly survive) that individuals having any advantage, however slight, over others, would have the best chance of surviving and of procreating their kind? On the other hand, we may feel sure that any variation in the least degree injurious would be rigidly destroyed. This preservation of favorable individual differences and variations, and the destruction of those which are injurious, I have called Natural Selection, or the Survival of the Fittest. Variations neither useful nor injurious would not be affected by natural selection, and would be left either a fluctuating element, as perhaps we see in certain polymorphic species, or would ultimately become fixed, owing to the nature of the organism and the nature of the conditions.

Several writers have misapprehended or objected to the term Natural Selection. Some have even imagined that natural selection induces variability, whereas it implies only the preservation of such variations as arise and are beneficial to the being under its conditions of life. No one objects to agriculturists speaking of the potent effects of man's selection: and in this case, the individual differences given by nature, which man for some object selects, must of necessity first occur. Others have objected that the term selection implies conscious choice in the animals which become modified; and it has even been urged that, as plants have no volition, natural selection is not applicable to them! In the literal sense of the word, no doubt, natural selection is a false term; but whoever objected to chemists speaking of the elective affinities of the various elements?—and yet an acid cannot strictly be said to elect the base with which it in preference combines. It has been said that I speak of natural selection as an active power or Deity; but who objects to an author speaking of the attraction of gravity as ruling the movements of the planets? Everyone knows what is meant and is implied by such metaphorical expressions; and they are almost necessary for brevity. So again it is difficult to avoid personifying the word Nature; but I mean by Nature, only the aggregate action and product of many natural laws, and by laws the sequence of events as ascertained by us. With a little familiarity such superficial objections will be forgotten.

* * *

As man can produce, and certainly has produced, a great result by his methodical and unconscious means of selection, what may not natural selection effect? Man can act only on external and visible characters: Nature, if I may be allowed to personify the natural preservation or survival of the fittest, cares nothing for appearance, except in so far as they are useful to any being. She can act on every internal organ, on every shade of constitutional difference, on the whole machinery of life. Man selects only for his own good: Nature only for that of the being which she tends. Every selected character is fully exercised by her, as is implied by the fact of their selection. Man keeps the native of many climates in the same country; he seldom exercises each selected character in some peculiar and fitting manner; he feeds a long- and a short-beaked pigeon on the same food; he does not exercise a long-backed or long-legged quadruped in any peculiar manner; he exposes sheep with long and short wool to the same climate. He does not allow the most vigorous males to struggle for the females. He does not rigidly destroy all inferior animals, but protects during each varying season, as far as lies in his power, all his productions. He often begins his selection by some half-monstrous form; or at least by some modification prominent enough to catch the eye or to be plainly useful to him. Under nature, the slightest differences of structure or constitution may well turn the nicely balanced scale in the struggle for life, and so be preserved. How fleeting are the wishes and efforts of man! how short his time! and consequently how poor will be his results, compared with those accumulated by Nature during whole geological periods! Can we wonder, then, that Nature's productions should be far "truer" in character than man's productions; that they should be infinitely better adapted to the most complex conditions of life, and should plainly bear the stamp of far higher workmanship?

* * *

That natural selection generally acts with extreme slowness I fully admit. It can act only when there are places in the natural polity of a district which can be better occupied by the modification of some of its existing inhabitants. The occurrence of such places will often depend on physical changes, which generally take place very slowly, and on the immigration of better adapted forms being prevented. As some few of the old inhabitants become modified, the mutual relations of others will often be disturbed; and this will create new places, ready to be filled up by better adapted forms; but all this will take place very slowly. Although all the individuals of the same species differ in some slight degree from each other, it would often be long before differences of the right nature in various parts of the organization might occur. The result would often be greatly retarded by free intercrossing. Many will exclaim that these several causes are amply sufficient to neutralize the power of natural selection. I do not believe so. But I do believe that natural selection will generally act very slowly, only at long intervals of time, and only on a few of the inhabitants of the same region. I further believe that these slow, intermittent results accord well with what geology tells us of the rate and manner at which the inhabitants of the world have changed.

* * *

Natural selection acts solely through the preservation of variations in some way advantageous, which consequently endure. Owing to the high geometrical rate of increase of all organic beings, each area is already fully stocked with inhabitants; and it follows from this, that as the favored forms increase in number, so, generally, will the less favored decrease and become rare. Rarity, as geology tells us, is the precursor to extinction. We can see that any form which is represented by few individuals will run a good chance of utter extinction, during great fluctuations in the nature of the seasons, or from a temporary increase in the number of its enemies. But we may go further than this; for, as new forms are produced, unless we admit that specific forms can go on indefinitely increasing in number, many old forms must become extinct. That the number of specific forms has not indefinitely increased, geology plainly tells us; and we shall presently attempt to show why it is that the number of species throughout the world has not become immeasurably great.

We have seen that the species which are most numerous in individuals have the best chance of producing favorable variations within any given period. We have evidence of this, in the facts stated in the second chapter, showing that it is the common and diffused or dominant species which offer the greatest number of recorded varieties. Hence, rare species will be less quickly modified or improved within any given period; they will consequently be beaten in the race for life by the modified and improved descendants of the commoner species.

From these several considerations I think it inevitably follows, that as new species in the course of time are formed through natural selection, others will become rarer and rarer, and finally extinct. The forms which stand in closest competition, with those undergoing modification and improvement, will naturally suffer most. And we have seen in the chapter on the Struggle for Existence that it is the most closely allied forms—varieties of the same species, and species of the same genus or of related genera—which, from having nearly the same structure, constitution, and habits, generally come into the severest competition with each other; consequently, each new variety or species, during the progress of its formation, will generally press hardest on its nearest kindred, and tend to exterminate them. We see the same process of extermination amongst our domesticated productions, through the selection of improved forms by man. Many curious instances could be given showing how quickly new breeds of cattle, sheep, and other animals, and varieties of flowers, take the place of older and inferior kinds. In Yorkshire, it is historically known that the ancient black cattle were displaced by the longhorns, and that these were "swept away by the shorthorns" (I quote the words of an agricultural writer) "as if by some murderous pestilence."

CHAPTER XV

Recapitulation and Conclusion

It can hardly be supposed that a false theory would explain, in so satisfactory a manner as does the theory of natural selection, the several large classes of facts above specified. It has recently been objected that this is an unsafe method of arguing; but it is a method used in judging of the common events of life, and has often been used by the greatest natural philosophers. The undulatory theory of light has thus been arrived at; and the belief in the revolution of the earth on its own axis was until lately supported by hardly any direct evidence. It is no valid objection that science as yet throws no light on the far higher problem of the essence or origin of life. Who can explain what is the essence of the attraction of gravity? No one now objects to following out the results consequent on this unknown element of attraction; notwithstanding that Leibnitz formerly accused Newton of introducing "occult qualities and miracles into philosophy."

I see no good reason why the views given in this volume should shock the religious feelings of anyone. It is satisfactory, as showing how transient such impressions are, to remember that the greatest discovery ever made by man—namely, the law of the attraction of gravity—was also attacked by Leibnitz, "as subversive of natural and inferentially of revealed, religion." A celebrated author and divine has written to me that "he has gradually learnt to see that it is just as noble a conception of the Deity to believe that He created a few original forms capable of self-development into other and needful forms, as to believe that He required a fresh act of creation to supply the voids caused by the action of His Laws."

Why, it may be asked, until recently did nearly all the most eminent living naturalist and geologists disbelieve in the mutability of species? It cannot be asserted that organic beings in a state of nature are subject to no variation; it cannot be proved that the amount of variation in the course of long ages is a limited quantity; no clear distinction has been, or can be, drawn between species and well-marked varieties. It cannot be maintained that species when intercrossed are invariably sterile, and varieties invariably fertile; or that sterility is a special endowment and sign of creation. The belief that species were immutable productions was almost unavoidable as long as the history of the world was thought to be of short duration; and now that we have acquired some idea of the lapse of time, we are too apt to assume, without proof, that the geological record is so perfect that it would have afforded us plain evidence of the mutation of species, if they had undergone mutation.

But the chief cause of our natural unwillingness to admit that one species has given birth to other and distinct species, is that we are always slow in admitting great changes of which we do not see the steps. The difficulty is the same as that felt by so many geologists, when Lyell first insisted that long lines of inland cliffs had been formed, and great valleys excavated, by the agencies which we see still at work. The mind cannot possibly grasp the full meaning of the term of even a million years; it cannot add up and perceive the full effects of many slight variations, accumulated during an almost infinite number of generations.

* * *

Analogy would lead me one step farther; namely, to the belief that all animals and plants are descended from someone prototype. But analogy may be a deceitful guide. Nevertheless all living things have much in common, in their chemical composition, their cellular structure, their laws of growth, and their liability to injurious influences. We see this even in so trifling a fact as that the same poison often similarly affects plants and animals; or that the poison secreted by the gallfly produces monstrous growths on the wild rose or oak tree. With all organic beings, excepting perhaps some of the very lowest, sexual reproduction seems to be essentially similar. With all, as far as is at present known, the germinal vesicle is the same; so that all organisms start from a common origin. If we look even to the two main divisions—namely, to the animal and vegetable kingdoms—certain low forms are so far intermediate in character that naturalists have disputed to which kingdom they should be referred. As Professor Asa Gray has remarked, "the spores and other reproductive bodies of many of the lower algae may claim to have first a characteristically animal, and then an unequivocally vegetable existence." Therefore, on the principle of natural selection with divergence of character, it does not seem incredible that, from some such low and intermediate form, both animals and plants may have been developed; and, if we admit this, we must likewise admit that all the organic beings which have ever lived on this earth may be descended from some one primordial form. But this inference is chiefly grounded on analogy, and it is immaterial whether or not it be accepted. No doubt it is possible, as Mr. G. H. Lewes has urged, that at the first commencement of life many different forms were evolved; but if so, we may conclude that only a very few have left modified descendants. For, as I have recently remarked in regard to the members of each great kingdom, such as the Vertebrata, Articulata, &c., we have distinct evidence in their embryological, homologous, and rudimentary structures, that within each kingdom all the members are descended from a single progenitor.

Language

Ralph Waldo Emerson

Language is the third use which nature subserves to man. Nature is the vehicle of thought, and in a simple, double, and three-fold degree.

1. Words are signs of natural facts.

2. Particular natural facts are symbols of particular spiritual facts.

3. Nature is the symbol of spirit.

   1. Words are signs of natural facts. The use of natural history is to give us aid in supernatural history; the use of the outer creation, to give us language for the beings and changes of the inward creation. Every word which is used to express a moral or intellectual fact, if traced to its root, is found to be borrowed from some material appearance. *Right* means *straight*; *wrong* means *twisted*. *Spirit* primarily means wind; *transgression*, the crossing of a line; *supercilious*, the *raising of the eyebrow*. We say the *heart* to express emotion, the *head* to denote thought; and *thought* and *emotion* are words borrowed from sensible things, and now appropriated to spiritual nature. Most of the process by which this transformation is made, is hidden from us in the remote time when language was framed; but the same tendency may be daily observed in children. Children and savages use only nouns or names of things, which they convert into verbs, and apply to analogous mental acts.

   2. But this origin of all words that convey spiritual import—so conspicuous a fact in the history of language—is our least debt to nature. It is not words only that are emblematic; it is things which are emblematic. Every natural fact is a symbol of some spiritual fact. Every appearance in nature corresponds to some state of the mind, and that state of the mind can only be described by presenting that natural appearance as its picture. An enraged man is a lion, a cunning man is a fox, a firm man is a rock, and a learned man is a torch. A lamb is innocence; a snake is subtle spite; flowers express to us the delicate affections. Light and darkness are our familiar expression for knowledge and ignorance; and heat for love. Visible distance, behind and before us, is respectively our image of memory and hope.

Who looks upon a river in a meditative hour and is not reminded of the flux of all things? Throw a stone into the stream, and the circles that propagate themselves are the beautiful type of all influence. Man is conscious of a universal soul within or behind his individual life, wherein, as in a firmament, the natures of Justice, Truth, Love, Freedom, arise and shine. This universal soul he calls Reason: it is not mine, or thine, or his, but we are its; we are its property and men. And the blue sky in which the private earth is buried, the sky with its eternal calm, and full of everlasting orbs, is the type of Reason. That which

Source: Ralph Waldo Emerson, 1836.

intellectually considered we call Reason, considered in relation to nature, we call Spirit. Spirit is the Creator. Spirit hath life in itself. And man in all ages and countries embodies it in his language as the FATHER.

It can easily be seen that there is nothing lucky or capricious in these analogies, but that they are constant, and pervade nature. These are not the dreams of a few poets, here and there, but man is an analogist, and studies relations in all objects. He is placed in the center of beings, and a ray of relation passes from every other being to him. And neither can man be understood without these objects, nor these objects without man. All the facts in natural history taken by themselves have no value, but are barren, like a single sex. But marry it to human history, and it is full of life. Whole floras, all Linnaeus' and Buffon's volumes, are dry catalogs of facts; but the most trivial of these facts, the habit of a plant, the organs, or work, or noise of an insect, applied to the illustration of a fact in intellectual philosophy, or in any way associated to human nature, affects us in the most lively and agreeable manner. The seed of a plant—to what affecting analogies in the nature of man is that little fruit made use of, in all discourse, up to the voice of Paul, who calls the human corpse a seed—"It is sown a natural body: it is raised a spiritual body." The motion of the earth round its axis and round the sun, makes the day and the year. These are certain amounts of brute light and heat. But is there no intent of an analogy between man's life and the seasons? And do the seasons gain no grandeur or pathos from that analogy? The instincts of the ant are very unimportant considered as the ant's; but the moment a ray of relation is seen to extend from it to man, and the little drudge is seen to be a monitor, a little body with a mighty heart, then all its habit, even that said to be recently observed, that it never sleeps, becomes sublime.

Because of this radical correspondence between visible things and human thoughts, savages, who have only what is necessary, converse in figures. As we go back in history, language becomes more picturesque, until its infancy, when it is all poetry; or all spiritual facts are represented by natural symbols. The same symbols are found to make the original elements of all languages. It has moreover been observed, that the idioms of all languages approach each other in passages of the greatest eloquence and power. And as this is the first language, so is it the last. This immediate dependence of language upon nature . . . never loses its power to affect us. It is this which gives that piquancy to the conversation of a strong-natured farmer or backwoodsman which all men relish.

A man's power to connect his thought with its proper symbol, and so to utter it, depends on the simplicity of his character, that is, upon his love of truth and his desire to communicate it without loss. The corruption of man is followed by the corruption of language. When simplicity of character and the sovereignty of ideas is broken up by the prevalence of secondary desires—the desire of riches, of pleasure, of power, and of praise—and duplicity and falsehood take place of simplicity and truth, the power over nature as an interpreter of the will is in a degree lost; new imagery ceases to be created, and old words are perverted to stand for things which are not; a paper currency is employed, when there is no bullion in the vaults. In due time, the fraud is manifest, and words lose all power to stimulate the understanding or the affections. Hundreds of writers may be found in every long-civilized nation who for a short time believe and make others believe that they see and utter truths, who do not of themselves clothe one thought in its natural garment, but who feed unconsciously on the language created by the primary writers of the country, those, namely, who hold primarily on nature.

An Essay Concerning Human Understanding (excerpted)

John Locke

1. It is an established opinion amongst some men, that there are in the understanding certain *innate principles*; some primary notions, characters, as it were stamped upon the mind of man, which the soul receives in its very first being; and brings into the world with it. It would be sufficient to convict unprejudiced readers of the falseness of this supposition, if I should only shew how men, barely by the use of their natural faculties, may attain to all the knowledge they have, without the help of any innate impressions; and may arrive at certainty, without any such original notions or principles.

* * *

2. Let us then suppose the mind to be, as we say, white paper, void of all characters, without any *ideas*; How comes it to be furnished? Whence comes it by that vast store, which the busy and boundless fancy of man has painted on it, with an almost endless variety? Whence has it all the materials of reason and knowledge? To this I answer, in one word, from *experience*: In that, all our knowledge is founded; and from that it ultimately derives itself. Our observation employed either about *external, sensible objects; or about the internal operations of our minds, perceived and reflected on by ourselves, is that, which supplies our understandings with all the materials of thinking.* These two are the fountains of knowledge, from whence all the *ideas* we have, or can naturally have, do spring . . .

5. The understanding seems to me, not to have the least glimmering of any *ideas,* which it doth not receive from one of these two. *External objects furnish the mind with the* ideas *of sensible qualities,* which are all those different perceptions they produce in us: And the *mind furnishes the understanding with* ideas *of its own operations* . . .

6. He that attentively considers the state of a *child,* at his first coming into the world, will have little reason to think him stored with plenty of *ideas* that are to be the matter of his future knowledge. 'Tis by degrees he comes to be furnished with them.

But all that are born into the world being surrounded with bodies, that perpetually and diversely affect them, variety of *ideas,* whether care be taken about it or no, are imprinted on the minds of children. *Light* and *colors* are busy at hand everywhere, when the eye is but open; *sounds* and some *tangible qualities* fail not to solicit their proper senses, and force an entrance to the mind; but yet, I think it will be granted easily, that if a child were kept in a place, where he never saw any other but black and white, till he were a man, he would have no more *ideas* of scarlet or green, than he that from his childhood never tasted an oyster, or a pineapple, has of those particular relishes.

Source: From *An Essay Concerning Human Understanding* by John Locke, 1689.

On Liberty

John Stuart Mill

The object of this essay is to assert one very simple principle, as entitled to govern absolutely the dealings of society with the individual in the way of compulsion and control, whether the means used by physical force in the form of legal penalties, or the moral coercion of public opinion. That principle is, that the sole end for which mankind are warranted, individually or collectively, in interfering with the liberty of action of any of their number, is self-protection. That the only purpose for which power can be rightfully exercised over any member of a civilized community, against his will, is to prevent harm to others. His own good, either physical or moral, is not a sufficient warrant. He cannot rightfully be compelled to do or forbear because it will be better for him to do so, because it will make him happier, because, in the opinions of others, to do so would be wise, or even right. These are good reasons for remonstrating with him, or reasoning with him, or persuading him, or entreating him, but not for compelling him, or visiting him with any evil in case he do otherwise. To justify that, the conduct from which it is desired to deter him, must be calculated to produce evil to someone else. The only part of the conduct of any one, for which he is amenable to society, is that which concerns others. In the part which merely concerns himself, his independence is, of right, absolute. Over himself, over his own body and mind, the individual is sovereign.

It is, perhaps, hardly necessary to say that this doctrine is meant to apply only to human beings in the maturity of their faculties. We are not speaking of children, or of young persons below the age which the law may fix as that of manhood or womanhood. Those who are still in a state to require being taken care of by others, must be protected against their own actions as well as against external injury . . .

But there is a sphere of action in which society, as distinguished from the individual, has, if any, only an indirect interest; comprehending all that portion of a person's life and conduct which affects only himself, or it is also affects others, only with their free, voluntary, and undeceived consent and participation. When I say only himself, I mean directly, and in the first instance: for whatever affects himself, may affect others through himself; and the objection which may be grounded on this contingency will receive consideration in the sequel. This, then, is the appropriate region of human liberty. It comprises, first, the inward domain of consciousness; demanding liberty of conscience, in the most comprehensive sense; liberty of thought and feeling; absolute freedom of opinion and sentiment on all subjects, practical or speculative, scientific, moral, or theological. The liberty of expressing and publishing opinions may seem to fall under a different principle, since it belongs to that part of the conduct of an individual which concerns other people; but, being almost of as much importance as the liberty of thought itself, and resting in great part on the same reasons, is practically inseparable from it.

Source: From *Utilitarianism* by John Stuart Mill, 1859.

Secondly, the principle requires liberty of tastes and pursuits; of framing the plan of our life to suit our own character; of doing as we like, subject to such consequences as may follow: without impediment from our fellow creatures, so long as what we do does not harm them, even though they should think our conduct foolish, perverse, or wrong. Thirdly, from this liberty of each individual, follows the liberty, within the same limits, of combination among individuals; freedom to unite, for any purpose not involving harm to others: the persons combining being supposed to be of full age, and not forced or deceived.

No society in which these liberties are not, on the whole, respected, is free, whatever may be its form of government; and none is completely free in which they do not exist absolute and unqualified. The only freedom which deserves the name, is that of pursuing our own good in our own way, so long as we do not attempt to deprive others of theirs, or impede their efforts to obtain it. Each is the proper guardian of his own health, whether bodily, or mental and spiritual. Mankind are greater gainers by suffering each other to live as seems good to themselves, than by compelling each to live as seems good to the rest . . .

On the Liberty of Thought and Discussion

. . . If all mankind minus one, were of one opinion, and only one person were of the contrary opinion, mankind would be no more justified in silencing that one person, than he, if he had the power, would be justified in silencing mankind. Were an opinion a personal possession of no value except to the owner; if to be obstructed in the enjoyment of it were simply a private injury, it would make some difference whether the injury was inflicted only on a few persons or on many. But the peculiar evil of silencing the expression of an opinion is, that it is robbing the human race; posterity as well as the existing generation; those who dissent form the opinion, still more than those who hold it. If the opinion is right, they are deprived of the opportunity of exchanging error for truth: if wrong, they lose, what is almost as great a benefit, the clearer perception and livelier impression of truth, produced by its collision with error.

It is necessary to consider separately these two hypotheses, each of which has a distinct branch of the argument corresponding to it. We can never be sure that the opinion we are endeavoring to stifle is a false opinion; and if we were sure, stifling it would be an evil still.

First, the opinion which it is attempted to suppress by authority may possibly be true. Those who desire to suppress it, of course deny its truth; but they are not infallible. They have no authority to decide the question for all mankind, and exclude every other person from the means of judging. To refuse a hearing to an opinion, because they are sure that it is false, is to assume that *their* certainty is the same thing as *absolute* certainty. All silencing of discussion is an assumption of infallibility. Its condemnation may be allowed to rest on this common argument, not the worse for being common.

Unfortunately for the good sense of mankind, the fact of their fallibility is far from carrying the weight in their practical judgment, which is always allowed to it in theory; for while everyone well knows himself to be fallible, few think it necessary to take any precautions against their own fallibility, or admit the supposition that any opinion, of which they feel very certain, may be one of the examples of the error to which they acknowledge themselves to be liable . . .

Let us now pass to the second division of the argument, and dismissing the supposition that any of the received opinions may be false, let us assume them to be true, and examine into the worth of the manner in which they are likely to be held, when their truth is not freely and openly canvassed. However unwillingly a person who has a strong opinion may admit the possibility that his opinion may be false, he ought to be moved by the consideration that however true it may be, if it is not fully, frequently, and fearlessly discussed, it will be held as a dead dogma, not a living truth.

There is a class of persons (happily not quite so numerous as formerly) who think it enough if a person assents undoubtingly to what they think true, though he has no knowledge whatever of the grounds of the opinion, and could not make a tenable defense of it against the most superficial objections. Such persons, if they can once get their creed taught from authority, naturally think that no good, and some harm, comes of it being allowed to be questioned. Where their influence prevails, they make it nearly impossible for the received opinion to be rejected wisely and considerately, though it may still be rejected rashly and ignorantly; for to shut out discussion entirely is seldom possible, and when it once gets in, beliefs not grounded on conviction are apt to give way before the slightest semblance of an argument. Waiving, however, this possibility—assuming that the true opinion abides in the mind, but abides as a prejudice, a belief independent of, and proof against, argument—this is not the way in which truth ought to be held by a rational being. This is not knowing the truth. Truth, thus held, is but one superstition the more, accidentally clinging to the words which enunciate a truth.

If the intellect and judgment of mankind ought to be cultivated, a thing which Protestants at least do not deny, on what can these faculties be more appropriately exercised by any one, than on the things which concern him so much that it is considered necessary for him to hold opinions on them? If the cultivation of the understanding consists in one thing more than in another, it is surely in learning the grounds of one's own opinions. Whatever people believe, on subjects on which it is of the first importance to believe rightly, they ought to be able to defend against at least the common objections. But, someone may say, "Let them be *taught* the grounds of their opinions." It does not follow that opinions must be merely parroted because they are never heard controverted. Persons who learn geometry do not simply commit the theorems to memory, but understand and learn likewise the demonstrations; and it would be absurd to say that they remain ignorant of the grounds of geometrical truths, because they never hear any one deny, and attempt to disprove them. Undoubtedly, and such teaching suffices on a subject like mathematics, where there is nothing at all to be said on the wrong side of the question. The peculiarity of the evidence of mathematical truths is, that all the argument is on one side. There are no objections, and no answers to objections. But on every subject on which difference of opinion is possible, the truth depends on a balance to be struck between two sets of conflicting reasons . . . He who knows only his own side of the case, knows little of that. His reasons may be good, and no one may have been able to refute them. But if he is equally unable to refute the reasons on the opposite side; if he does not so much as know what they are, he has no ground for preferring either opinion. The rational position for him would be suspension of judgment, and unless he contents himself with that, he is either led by authority, or adopts, like the generality of the world, the side to which he feels most inclination. Nor is it enough that he should hear the arguments of adversaries from his own teachers, presented as they state them, and accompanied by what they offer as refutations. That is not the way to do justice to the arguments, or bring them into real contact with his own mind. He must be able to hear them from persons who actually believe them; who defend them in earnest, and do their very utmost for them. He must know them in their most plausible and persuasive form; he must feel the whole force of the difficulty which the true view of the subject has to encounter and dispose of; else he will never really possess himself of the portion of truth which meets and removes that difficulty . . .

. . . The fact, however, is, that not only the grounds of the opinion are forgotten in the absence of discussion, but too often the meaning of the opinion itself. The words which convey it, cease to suggest ideas, or suggest only a small portion of those they were originally employed to communicate. Instead of a vivid conception and a living belief, there remain only a few phrases retained by rote; or, if any part, the shell and husk only of the meaning is retained, the finer essence being lost. The great chapter in human history which this fact occupies and fills, cannot be too earnestly studied and meditated on.

It is illustrated in the experience of almost all ethical doctrines and religious creeds. They are all full of meaning and vitality to those who originate them, and to the direct disciples of the originators. Their meaning continues to be felt in undiminished strength, and is perhaps brought out into even fuller consciousness, so long as the struggle lasts to give the doctrine or creed an ascendancy over other creeds. At last it either prevails, and becomes the general opinion, or its progress stops; it keeps possession of the ground it has gained, but ceases to spread further. When either of these results has become apparent, controversy on the subject flags, and gradually dies away . . .

It still remains to speak of one of the principal causes which make diversity of opinion advantageous, and will continue to do so until mankind shall have entered a stage of intellectual advancement which at present seems at an incalculable distance. We have hitherto considered only two possibilities: that the received opinion may be false, and some other opinion, consequently, true; or that, the received opinion being true, a conflict with the opposite error is essential to a clear apprehension and deep feeling of its truth. But there is a commoner case than either of these; when the conflicting doctrines, instead of being one true and the other false, share the truth between them; and the nonconforming opinion is needed to supply the remainder of the truth, of which the received doctrine embodies only a part. Popular opinions, on subjects not palpable to sense, are often true, but seldom or never the whole truth. They are a part of the truth; sometimes a greater, sometimes a smaller part, but exaggerated, distorted, and disjoined from the truths by which they ought to be accompanied and limited. Heretical opinions, on the other hand, are generally some of these suppressed and neglected truths, bursting the bonds which kept them down, and either seeking reconciliation with the truth contained in the common opinion, or fronting it as enemies, and setting themselves up, with similar exclusiveness, as the whole truth. The latter case is hitherto the most frequent, as, in the human mind, one-sidedness has always been the rule, and many-sidedness the exception. Hence, even in revolutions of opinion, one part of the truth usually sets while another rises. Even progress, which ought to superadd, for the most part only substitutes, one partial and incomplete truth for another; improvement consisting chiefly in this, that the new fragment of truth is more wanted, more adapted to the needs of the time, than that which it displaces. Such being the partial character of prevailing opinions, even when resting on a true foundation, every opinion which embodies somewhat of the portion of truth which the common opinion omits, ought to be considered precious, with whatever amount of error and confusion that truth may be blended. No sober judge of human affairs will feel bound to be indignant because those who force on our notice truths which we should otherwise have overlooked, overlook some of those which we see. Rather, he will think that so long as popular truth is one-sided, it is more desirable than otherwise that unpopular truth should have one-sided asserters too; such being usually the most energetic, and the most likely to compel reluctant attention to the fragment of wisdom which they proclaim as if it were the whole . . .

We have now recognized the necessity to the mental well-being of mankind (on which all their other well-being depends) of freedom of opinion, and freedom of the expression of opinion, on four distinct grounds; which we will now briefly recapitulate.

First, if any opinion is compelled to silence, that opinion may, for aught we can certainly know, be true. To deny this is to assume our own infallibility.

Secondly, though the silenced opinion be an error, it may, and very commonly does, contain a portion of truth; and since the general or prevailing opinion on any subject is rarely or never the whole truth, it is only by the collision of adverse opinions that the remainder of the truth has any chance of being supplied.

Thirdly, even if the received opinion be not only true, but the whole truth; unless it is suffered to be, and actually is, vigorously and earnestly contested, it will, by most of those who receive it, be held in the manner of a prejudice, with little comprehension or feeling of its rational grounds. And not only this, but, fourthly, the meaning of the doctrine itself will be in danger of being lost, or enfeebled, and deprived of its vital effect on the character and conduct: the dogma becoming a mere formal profession, inefficacious for good, but cumbering the ground, and preventing the growth of any real and heartfelt conviction, from reason or personal experience . . .

Politics and the English Language

George Orwell

MOST PEOPLE WHO BOTHER with the matter at all would admit that the English language is in a bad way, but it is generally assumed that we cannot by conscious action do anything about it. Our civilization is decadent, and our language—so the argument runs—must inevitably share in the general collapse. It follows that any struggle against the abuse of language is a sentimental archaism, like preferring candles to electric light or hansom cabs to airplanes. Underneath this lies the half-conscious belief that language is a natural growth and not an instrument which we shape for our own purposes.

Now, it is clear that the decline of a language must ultimately have political and economic causes: it is not due simply to the bad influence of this or that individual writer. But an effect can become a cause, reinforcing the original cause and producing the same effect in an intensified form, and so on, indefinitely. A man may take to drink because he feels himself to be a failure, and then fail all the more completely because he drinks. It is rather the same thing that is happening to the English language. It becomes ugly and inaccurate because our thoughts are foolish, but the slovenliness of our language makes it easier for us to have foolish thoughts. The point is that the process is reversible. Modern English, especially written English, is full of bad habits which spread by imitation and which can be avoided if one is willing to take the necessary trouble. If one gets rid of these habits, one can think more clearly, and to think clearly is a necessary first step toward political regeneration: so that the fight against bad English is not frivolous and is not the exclusive concern of professional writers. I will come back to this presently, and I hope that by that time the meaning of what I have said here will have become clearer. Meanwhile, here are five specimens of the English language as it is now habitually written.

These five passages have not been picked out because they are especially bad—I could have quoted far worse if I had chosen—but because they illustrate various of the mental vices from which we now suffer. They are a little below the average, but are fairly representative samples. I number them so that I can refer back to them when necessary:

1. I am not, indeed, sure whether it is not true to say that the Milton who once seemed not unlike a seventeenth-century Shelley had not become, out of an experience ever more bitter in each year, more alien (sic) to the founder of that Jesuit sect which nothing could induce him to tolerate.

   PROFESSOR HAROLD LASKI
   (Essay in Freedom of Expression)

2. Above all, we cannot play ducks and drakes with a native battery of idioms which prescribes such egregious collocations of vocables as the basic *put up with* for *tolerate* or *put at a loss* for *bewilder*.

   PROFESSOR LANCELOT HOGBEN
   (Interglossa)

3. On the one side, we have the free personality; by definition it is not neurotic, for it has neither conflict nor dream. Its desires, such as they are, are transparent, for they are just what institutional approval keeps in the forefront of consciousness; another institutional pattern would alter their number and intensity; there is little in them that is natural, irreducible, or culturally dangerous. But on the other side, the social bond itself is nothing but the mutual reflection of these self-secure integrities. Recall the definition of love. Is not this the very picture of a small academic? Where is there a place in this hall of mirrors for either personality or fraternity?

   ESSAY ON PSYCHOLOGY in Politics
   (New York)

4. All the "best people" from the gentlemen's clubs, and all the frantic fascist captains, united in common hatred of socialism and bestial horror of the rising tide of the mass revolutionary movement, have turned to acts of provocation, to foul incendiarism, to medieval legends of poisoned wells, to legalize their own destruction of proletarian organizations, and rouse the agitated petty bourgeoisie to chauvinistic fervor on behalf of the fight against the revolutionary way out of the crisis.

   COMMUNIST PAMPHLET

5. If a new spirit is to be infused into this old country, there is one thorny and contentious reform which must be tackled, and that is the humanization and galvanization of the B.B.C. Timidity here will bespeak canker and atrophy of the soul. The heart of Britain may lee sound and of strong beat, for instance, but the British lion's roar at present is like that of Bottom in Shakespeare's Midsummer Night's Dream—as gentle as any sucking dove. A virile new Britain cannot continue indefinitely to be traduced in the eyes, or rather ears, of the world by the effete languors of Langham Place, brazenly masquerading as "standard English." When the voice of Britain is heard at nine o'clock, better far and infinitely less ludicrous to hear aitches honestly dropped than the present priggish, inflated, inhibited, school-ma'am-ish arch braying of blameless bashful mewing maidens.

   LETTER IN Tribune

Each of these passages has faults of its own, but quite apart from avoidable ugliness, two qualities are common to all of them. The first is staleness of imagery; the other is lack of precision. The writer either has a meaning and cannot express it, or he inadvertently says something else, or he is almost indifferent as to whether his words mean anything or not.

This mixture of vagueness and sheer incompetence is the most marked characteristic of modern English prose, and especially of any kind of political writing. As soon as certain topics are raised, the concrete melts into the abstract and no one seems able to think of turns of speech that are not hackneyed: prose consists less and less of words chosen for the sake of their meaning, and more and more of phrases tacked together like the sections of a prefabricated henhouse. I list below, with notes and examples, various of the tricks by means of which the work of prose-construction is habitually dodged:

Dying metaphors. A newly invented metaphor assists thought by evoking a visual image, while on the other hand, a metaphor which is technically "dead" (e.g., iron resolution) has in effect reverted to being an ordinary word and can generally be used without loss of vividness. But in between these two classes, there is a huge dump of worn-out metaphors which have lost all evocative power and are merely used because they save people the trouble of inventing phrases for themselves. Examples are ring the changes on, take up the cudgels for, toe the line, ride roughshod over, stand shoulder to shoulder with, play into the hands of, an axe to grind, grist to the mill, fishing in troubled waters, on the order of the day, Achilles' heel, swan song, hotbed. Many of these are used without knowledge of their meaning (what is a "rift," for instance?), and incompatible metaphors are frequently mixed, a sure sign that the writer is not interested in what he is saying. Some metaphors now current have been twisted out of their original meaning without those who use them even being aware of the fact. For example, toe the line is sometimes written tow the line. Another example is the hammer and the anvil, now always used with the implication that the anvil gets the worst of it. In real life, it is always the anvil that breaks the hammer, never the other way about: a writer who stopped to think what he was saying would be aware of this, and would avoid perverting the original phrase.

Operators, or verbal false limbs. These save the trouble of picking out appropriate verbs and nouns, and at the same time pad each sentence with extra syllables which give it an appearance of symmetry. Characteristic phrases are render inoperative, militate against, prove unacceptable, make contact with, be subjected to, give rise to, give grounds for, having the effect of, play a leading part (role) in, make itself felt, take effect, exhibit a tendency to, serve the purpose of, and so forth. The keynote is the elimination of simple verbs. Instead of being a single word, such as break, stop, spoil, mend, kill, a verb becomes a phrase, made up of a noun or adjective tacked on to some general-purposes verb as prove, serve, form, play, render. In addition, the passive voice is wherever possible used in preference to the active, and noun constructions are used instead of gerunds (by examination of instead of by examining). The range of verbs is further cut down by means of the -ize and de- formations, and banal statements are given an appearance of profundity by means of the not un- formation. Simple conjunctions and prepositions are replaced by such phrases as with respect to, having regard to, the fact that, by dint of, in view of, in the interests of, on the hypothesis that; and the ends of sentences are saved from anticlimax by such resounding commonplaces as greatly to be desired, cannot be left out of account, a development to be expected in the near future, deserving of serious consideration, brought to a satisfactory conclusion, and so forth.

Pretentious diction. Words like phenomenon, element, individual (as noun), objective, categorical, effective, virtual, basis, primary, promote, constitute, exhibit, exploit, utilize, eliminate, liquidate, are used to dress up simple statements and give an air of scientific impartiality to biased judgments. Adjectives like epoch-making, epic, historic, unforgettable, triumphant, age-old, inevitable, inexorable, veritable, are used to dignify the sordid processes of international politics, while writing that aims at glorifying war usually takes on an archaic color, its characteristic words being: realm, throne, chariot, mailed fist, trident, sword, shield, buckler, banner, jackboot, clarion. Foreign words and expressions such as cul de sac, ancien regime, deus ex machina, mutatis mutandis, status quo, gleichschaltung, weltanschauung, are used to give an air of culture and elegance. Except for the useful abbreviations i.e., e.g., and etc., there is no real need for any of the hundreds of foreign phrases now current in English. Bad writers, and especially scientific, political and sociological writers, are nearly always haunted by the notion that Latin or Greek words are grander than Saxon ones, and unnecessary words like expedite, ameliorate, predict, extraneous, deracinated, clandestine, subaqueous and hundreds of others constantly gain ground from their Anglo-Saxon opposite numbers. The jargon peculiar to Marxist writing (hyena, hangman, cannibal, petty bourgeois, these gentry, lackey, flunkey, mad dog, White Guard, etc.) consists largely of words and phrases translated from Russian, German, or French; but the normal way of coining a new word is to use a Latin or Greek root with the appropriate affix and, where necessary, the -ize formation. It is often easier to make up words of this kind (deregionalize, impermissible, extramarital, nonfragmentary, etc.) than to think up the English words that will cover one's meaning. The result, in general, is an increase in slovenliness and vagueness. An interesting illustration of this is the way in which the English flower names which were in use till very recently are being ousted by Greek ones, snapdragon becoming antirrhinum, forget-me-not becoming myosotis, and so forth. It is hard to see any practical reason for this change of fashion: it is probably due to an instinctive turning away from the more homely word and a vague feeling that the Greek word is scientific.

Meaningless words. In certain kinds of writing, particularly in art criticism and literary criticism, it is normal to come across long passages which are almost completely lacking in meaning. Words like romantic, plastic, values, human, dead, sentimental, natural, vitality, as used in art criticism, are strictly meaningless, in the sense that they not only do not point to any discoverable object, but are hardly even expected to do so by the reader. When one critic writes, "The outstanding feature of Mr. X's work is its living quality," while another writes, "The immediately striking thing about Mr. X's work is its peculiar deadness," the reader accepts this as a simple difference of opinion. If words like black and white were involved, instead of the jargon words dead and living, he would see at once that language was being used in an improper way. Many political words are similarly abused. The word Fascism has now no meaning except in so far as it signifies "something not desirable." The words democracy, socialism, freedom, patriotic, realistic, justice, have each of them several different meanings which cannot be reconciled with one another. In the case of a word like democracy, not only is there no agreed definition, but the attempt to make one is resisted from all sides. It is almost universally felt that when we call a country democratic, we are praising it: consequently the defenders of every kind of régime claim that it is a democracy, and fear that they might have to stop using the word if it were tied down to any one meaning. Words of this kind are often used in a consciously dishonest way. That is, the person who uses them has his own private definition, but allows his hearer to think he means something quite different. Statements like Marshal Pétain was a true patriot, The Soviet Press is the freest in the world, The Catholic Church is opposed to persecution, are almost always made with intent to deceive. Other words used in variable meanings, in most cases more or less dishonestly, are class, totalitarian, science, progressive, reactionary bourgeois, equality.

Now that I have made this catalogue of swindles and perversions, let me give another example of the kind of writing that they lead to. This time it must of its nature be an imaginary one. I am going to translate a passage of good English into modern English of the worst sort. Here is a well-known verse from Ecclesiastes:

> I returned, and saw under the sun, that the race is not to the swift, nor the battle to the strong, neither yet bread to the wise, nor yet riches to men of understanding, nor yet favor to men of skill; but time and chance happened to them all.

Here it is in modern English:

> Objective consideration of contemporary phenomena compels the conclusion that success or failure in competitive activities exhibits no tendency to be commensurate with innate capacity, but that a considerable element of the unpredictable must invariably be taken into account.

This is a parody, but not a very gross one. Exhibit (3), above, for instance, contains several patches of the same kind of English. It will be seen that I have not made a full translation. The beginning and ending of the sentence follow the original meaning fairly closely, but in the middle the concrete illustrations—race, battle, bread—dissolve into the vague phrase "success or failure in competitive activities." This had to be so, because no modern writer of the kind I am discussing—no one capable of using phrases like objective consideration of contemporary phenomena—would ever tabulate his thoughts in that precise and detailed way. The whole tendency of modern prose is away from concreteness.

Now analyze these two sentences a little more closely. The first contains forty-nine words but only sixty syllables, and all its words are those of everyday life. The second contains thirty-eight words of ninety syllables: eighteen of its words are from Latin roots, and one from Greek. The first sentence contains six vivid images, and only one phrase ("time and chance") that could be called vague. The second contains not a single fresh, arresting phrase, and in spite of its ninety syllables it gives only a shortened version of the meaning contained in the first. Yet without a doubt, it is the second kind of sentence that is gaining ground in modern English. I do not want to exaggerate. This kind of writing is not yet universal, and outcrops of simplicity will occur here and there in the worst-written page. Still, if you or I were told to write a few lines on the uncertainty of human fortunes, we should probably come much nearer to my imaginary sentence than to the one from Ecclesiastes.

As I have tried to show, modern writing at its worst does not consist in picking out words for the sake of their meaning and inventing images in order to make the meaning clearer. It consists in gumming together long strips of words which have already been set in order by someone else, and making the results presentable by sheer humbug. The attraction of this way of writing is that it is easy. It is easier—even quicker, once you have the habit—to say in my opinion, it is a not unjustifiable assumption that than to say I think. If you use ready-made phrases, you not only don't have to hunt about for words; you also don't have to bother with the rhythms of your sentences, since these phrases are generally so arranged as to be more or less euphonious. When you are composing in a hurry—when you are dictating to a stenographer, for instance, or making a public speech—it is natural to fall into a pretentious, Latinized style. Tags like a consideration which we should do well to bear in mind or a conclusion to which all of us would readily assent will save many a sentence from coming down with a bump.

By using stale metaphors, similes and idioms, you save much mental effort at the cost of leaving your meaning vague, not only for your reader but for yourself. This is the significance of mixed metaphors. The sole aim of a metaphor is to call up a visual image. When these images clash—as in The Fascist octopus has sung its swan song, the jackboot is thrown into the melting pot—it can be taken as certain that the writer is not seeing a mental image of the objects he is naming; in other words, he is not really thinking. Look again at the examples I gave at the beginning of this essay. Professor Laski (1) uses five negatives in fifty-three words. One of these is superfluous, making nonsense of the whole passage, and in addition there is the slip alien for akin, making further nonsense, and several avoidable pieces of clumsiness which increase the general vagueness. Professor Hogben (2) plays ducks and drakes with a battery which is able to write prescriptions, and, while disapproving of the everyday phrase put up with, is unwilling to look egregious up in the dictionary and see what it means. (3), if one takes an uncharitable attitude toward it, is simply meaningless: probably one could work out its intended meaning by reading the whole of the article in which it occurs. In (4), the writer knows more or less what he wants to say, but an accumulation of stale phrases chokes him like tea leaves blocking a sink. In (5), words and meaning have almost parted company.

People who write in this manner usually have a general emotional meaning—they dislike one thing and want to express solidarity with another—but they are not interested in the detail of what they are saying. A scrupulous writer, in every sentence that he writes, will ask himself at least four questions, thus:

1. What am I trying to say?
2. What words will express it?
3. What image or idiom will make it clearer?
4. Is this image fresh enough to have an effect?

And he will probably ask himself two more:

1. Could I put it more shortly?
2. Have I said anything that is avoidably ugly?

But you are not obliged to go to all this trouble. You can shirk it by simply throwing your mind open and letting the ready-made phrases come crowding in. They will construct your sentences for you—even think your thoughts for you, to a certain extent—and at need they will perform the important service of partially concealing your meaning even from yourself. It is at this point that the special connection between politics and the debasement of language becomes clear.

In our time, it is broadly true that political writing is bad writing. Where it is not true, it will generally be found that the writer is some kind of rebel, expressing his private opinions and not a "party line." Orthodoxy, of whatever color, seems to demand a lifeless, imitative style. The political dialects to be found in pamphlets, leading articles, manifestoes, White Papers and the speeches of undersecretaries do, of course, vary from party to party, but they are all alike in that one almost never finds in them a fresh, vivid, homemade turn of speech. When one watches some tired hack on the platform mechanically repeating the familiar phrases—bestial atrocities, iron heel, bloodstained tyranny, free peoples of the world, stand shoulder to shoulder—one often has a curious feeling that one is not watching a live human being but some kind of dummy: a feeling which suddenly becomes stronger at moments when the light catches the speaker's spectacles and turns them into blank disks which seem to have no eyes behind them. And this is not altogether fanciful. A speaker who uses that kind of phraseology has gone some distance toward turning himself into a machine. The appropriate noises are coming out of his larynx, but his brain is not involved as it would be if he were choosing his words for himself. If the speech he is making is one that he is accustomed to make over and over again, he may be almost unconscious of what he is saying, as one is when one utters the responses in church. And this reduced state of consciousness, if not indispensable, is at any rate favorable to political conformity.

In our time, political speech and writing are largely the defense of the indefensible. Things like the continuance of British rule in India, the Russian purges and deportations, the dropping of the atom bombs on Japan, can indeed be defended, but only by arguments which are too brutal for most people to face, and which do not square with the professed aims of political parties. Thus political language has to consist largely of euphemism, question-begging, and sheer cloudy vagueness. Defenseless villages are bombarded from the air, the inhabitants driven out into the countryside, the cattle machine-gunned, the huts set on fire with incendiary bullets: this is called pacification. Millions of peasants are robbed of their farms and sent trudging along the roads with no more than they can carry: this is called transfer of population or rectification of frontiers. People are imprisoned for years without trial, or shot in the back of the neck or sent to die of scurvy in Arctic lumber camps: this is called elimination of unreliable elements. Such phraseology is needed if one wants to name things without calling up mental pictures of them.

Consider for instance some comfortable English professor defending Russian totalitarianism. He cannot say outright, "I believe in killing off your opponents when you can get good results by doing so." Probably, therefore, he will say something like this:

> While freely conceding that the Soviet régime exhibits certain features which the humanitarian may be inclined to deplore, we must, I think, agree that a certain curtailment of the right to political opposition is an unavoidable concomitant of transitional periods, and that the rigors which the Russian people have been called upon to undergo have been amply justified in the sphere of concrete achievement.

The inflated style is itself a kind of euphemism. A mass of Latin words falls upon the facts like soft snow, blurring the outlines and covering up all the details. The great enemy of clear language is insincerity. When there is a gap between one's real and one's declared aims, one turns, as it were instinctively, to long words and exhausted idioms, like a cuttlefish squirting out ink. In our age, there is no such thing as "keeping out of politics." All issues are political issues, and politics itself is a mass of lies, evasions, folly, hatred, and schizophrenia. When the general atmosphere is bad, language must suffer. I should expect to find—this is a guess which I have not sufficient knowledge to verify—that the German, Russian, and Italian languages have all deteriorated in the last ten or fifteen years as a result of dictatorship.

But if thought corrupts language, language can also corrupt thought. A bad usage can spread by tradition and imitation, even among people who should and do know better. The debased language that I have been discussing is in some ways very convenient. Phrases like a not unjustifiable assumption, leaves much to be desired, would serve no good purpose, a consideration which we should do well to bear in mind, are a continuous temptation, a packet of aspirins always at one's elbow. Look back through this essay, and for certain you will find that I have again and again committed the very faults I am protesting against. By this morning's post, I have received a pamphlet dealing with conditions in Germany. The author tells me that he "felt impelled" to write it. I open it at random, and here is almost the first sentence that I see: "[The Allies] have an opportunity not only of achieving a radical transformation of Germany's social and political structure in such a way as to avoid a nationalistic reaction in Germany itself, but at the same time of laying the foundations of a cooperative and unified Europe." You see, he "feels impelled" to write—feels, presumably, that he has something new to say—and yet his words, like cavalry horses answering the bugle, group themselves automatically into the familiar dreary pattern. This invasion of one's mind by ready-made phrases (lay the foundations, achieve a radical transformation) can only be prevented if one is constantly on guard against them, and every such phrase anesthetizes a portion of one's brain.

I said earlier that the decadence of our language is probably curable. Those who deny this would argue, if they produced an argument at all, that language merely reflects existing social conditions, and that we cannot influence its development by any direct tinkering with words and constructions. So far as the general tone or spirit of a politics and the language goes, this may be true, but it is not true in detail. Silly words and expressions have often disappeared, not through any evolutionary process but owing to the conscious action of a minority. Two recent examples were "exploring every avenue" and "leave no stone unturned," which were killed by the jeers of a few journalists. There is a long list of flyblown metaphors which could similarly be got rid of if enough people would interest themselves in the job; and it should also be possible to laugh the not unformation out of existence, 3 to reduce the amount of Latin and Greek in the average sentence, to drive out foreign phrases and strayed scientific words, and, in general, to make pretentiousness unfashionable. But all these are minor points. The defense of the English language implies more than this, and perhaps it is best to start by saying what it does not imply.

To begin with, it has nothing to do with archaism, with the salvaging of obsolete words and turns of speech, or with the setting up of a "standard English" which must never be departed from. On the contrary, it is especially concerned with the scrapping of every word or idiom which has outworn its usefulness. It has nothing to do with correct grammar and syntax, which are of no importance so long as one makes one's meaning clear, or with the avoidance of Americanisms, or with having what is called a "good prose style." On the other hand, it is not concerned with fake simplicity and the attempt to make written English colloquial. Nor does it even imply in every case preferring the Saxon word to the Latin one, though it does imply using the fewest and shortest words that will cover one's meaning. What is above all needed is to let the meaning choose the word, and not the other way about.

In prose, the worst thing one can do with words is to surrender them. When you think of a concrete object, you think wordlessly, and then, if you want to describe the thing, you have been visualizing, you probably hunt about till you find the exact words that seem to fit it. When you think of something abstract, you are more inclined to use words from the start, and unless you make a conscious effort to prevent it, the existing dialect will come rushing in and do the job for you, at the expense of blurring or even changing your meaning. Probably it is better to put off using words as long as possible and get one's meaning as clear as one can through pictures or sensations. Afterward one can choose—not simply accept—the phrases that will best cover the meaning, and then switch round and decide what impressions one's words are likely to make on another person. This last effort of the mind cuts out all stale or mixed images, all prefabricated phrases, needless repetitions, and humbug and vagueness generally.

But one can often be in doubt about the effect of a word or a phrase, and one needs rules that one can rely on when instinct fails. I think the following rules will cover most cases:

1. Never use a metaphor, simile, or other figure of speech which you are used to seeing in print.

2. Never use a long word where a short one will do.

3. If it is possible to cut a word out, always cut it out.

4. Never use the passive where you can use the active.

5. Never use a foreign phrase, a scientific word, or a jargon word if you can think of an everyday English equivalent.

6. Break any of these rules sooner than say anything barbarous.

These rules sound elementary, and so they are, but they demand a deep change of attitude in anyone who has grown used to writing in the style now fashionable. One could keep all of them and still write bad English, but one could not write the kind of stuff that I quoted in these five specimens at the beginning of this article.

I have not here been considering the literary use of language, but merely language as an instrument for expressing and not for concealing or preventing thought. Stuart Chase and others have come near to claiming that all abstract words are meaningless, and have used this as a pretext for advocating a kind of political quietism. Since you don't know what Fascism is, how can you struggle against Fascism? One need not swallow such absurdities as this, but one ought to recognize that the present political chaos is connected with the decay of language, and that one can probably bring about some improvement by starting at the verbal end. If you simplify your English, you are freed from the worst follies of orthodoxy. You cannot speak any of the necessary dialects, and when you make a stupid remark, its stupidity will be obvious, even to yourself. Political language—and with variations this is true of all political parties, from Conservatives to Anarchists—is designed to make lies sound truthful and murder respectable and to give an appearance of solidity to pure wind. One cannot change this all in a moment, but one can at least change one's own habits, and from time to time one can even, if one jeers loudly enough, send some worn out and useless phrase—some jackboot, Achilles' heel, hotbed, melting pot, acid test, veritable inferno, or other lump of verbal refuse—into the dustbin where it belongs.

The President's War Message
Franklin D. Roosevelt

Yesterday, December 7, 1941—a date which will live in infamy—the United States of America was suddenly and deliberately attacked by naval and air forces of the Empire of Japan.

The United States was at peace with that Nation and, at the solicitation of Japan, was still in conversation with its Government and its Emperor looking toward the maintenance of peace in the Pacific. Indeed, one hour after Japanese air squadrons had commenced bombing in Oahu, the Japanese Ambassador to the United States and his colleague delivered to the Secretary of State a formal reply to a recent American message. While this reply stated that it seemed useless to continue the existing diplomatic negotiations, it contained no threat or hint of war or armed attack.

It will be recorded that the distance of Hawaii from Japan makes it obvious that the attack was deliberately planned many days or even weeks ago. During the intervening time, the Japanese Government has deliberately sought to deceive the United States by false statements and expressions of hope for continued peace.

The attack yesterday on the Hawaiian Islands has caused severe damage to American naval and military forces. Very many American lives have been lost. In addition, American ships have been reported torpedoed on the high seas between San Francisco and Honolulu.

Yesterday the Japanese Government also launched an attack against Malaya.

Last night Japanese forces attacked Hong Kong.

Last night Japanese forces attacked Guam.

Last night Japanese forces attacked the Philippine Islands.

Last night the Japanese attacked Wake Island.

This morning the Japanese attacked Midway Island.

Japan has, therefore, undertaken a surprise offensive extending throughout the Pacific area. The facts of yesterday speak for themselves. The people of the United States have already formed their opinions and well understand the implications to the very life and safety of our Nation.

As Commander-in-Chief of the Army and Navy I have directed that all measures be taken for our defense.

Always will we remember the character of the onslaught against us.

No matter how long it may take us to overcome this premeditated invasion, the American people in their righteous might will win through to absolute victory.

Source: From Franklin D. Roosevelt, 1941.

I believe I interpret the will of the Congress and of the people when I assert that we will not only defend ourselves to the uttermost but will make very certain that this form of treachery shall never endanger us again.

Hostilities exist. There is no blinking at the fact that our people, our territory, and our interests are in grave danger.

With confidence in our armed forces—with the unbounded determination of our people—we will gain the inevitable triumph—so help us God.

I ask that the Congress declare that since the unprovoked and dastardly attack by Japan on Sunday, December 7th, a state of war has existed between the United States and the Japanese Empire.

A Modest Proposal

Jonathan Swift

For preventing the children of poor people in Ireland from being a burden to their parents or country, and for making them beneficial to the public.

It is a melancholy object to those who walk through this great town or travel in the country, when they see the streets, the roads, and cabin doors, crowded with beggars of the female-sex, followed by three, four, or six children, all in rags and importuning every passenger for an alms. These mothers, instead of being able to work for their honest livelihood, are forced to employ all their time in strolling to beg sustenance for their helpless infants, who, as they grow up, either turn thieves for want of work, or leave their dear native country to fight for the Pretender in Spain, or sell themselves to the Barbados.

I think it is agreed by all parties that this prodigious number of children in the arms, or on the backs, or at the heels of their mothers, and frequently of their fathers, is in the present deplorable state of the kingdom a very great additional grievance; and therefore whoever could find out a fair, cheap, and easy method of making these children sound, useful members of the commonwealth would deserve so well of the public as to have his statue set up for a preserver of the nation.

But my intention is very far from being confined to provide only for the children of professed beggars; it is of a much greater extent, and shall take in the whole number of infants at a certain age who are born of parents in effect as little able to support them as those who demand our charity in the streets.

As to my own part, having turned my thoughts for many years upon this important subject, and maturely weighed the several schemes of other projectors, I have always found them grossly mistaken in their computation. It is true, a child just dropped from its dam may be supported by her milk for a solar year, with little other nourishment; at most not above the value of two shillings, which the mother may certainly get, or the value in scraps, by her lawful occupation of begging; and it is exactly at one year old that I propose to provide for them in such a manner as instead of being a charge upon their parents or the parish, or wanting food and raiment for the rest of their lives, they shall on the contrary contribute to the feeding, and partly to the clothing, of many thousands.

There is likewise another great advantage in my scheme, that it will prevent those voluntary abortions, and that horrid practice of women murdering their bastard children, alas, too frequent among us, sacrificing the poor innocent babes, I doubt, more to avoid the expense than the shame, which would move tears and pity in the most savage and inhuman breast.

Source: From *A Modest Proposal* by Jonathan Swift, 1729.

The number of souls in this kingdom being usually reckoned one million and a half, of these I calculate there may be about two hundred thousand couple whose wives are breeders; from which number I subtract thirty thousand couples who are able to maintain their own children, although I apprehend there cannot be so many under the present distresses of the kingdom; but this being granted, there will remain an hundred and seventy thousand breeders. I again subtract fifty thousand for those women who miscarry, or whose children die by accident or disease within the year. There only remain an hundred and twenty thousand children of poor parents annually born. The question therefore is, how this number shall be reared and provided for, which, as I have already said, under the present situation of affairs, is utterly impossible by all the methods hitherto proposed. For we can neither employ them in handicraft or agriculture; we neither build houses (I mean in the country) nor cultivate land. They can very seldom pick up a livelihood by stealing till they arrive at six years old, except where they are of towardly parts; although I confess they learn the rudiments much earlier, during which time they can however be looked upon only as probationers, as I have been informed by a principal gentlemen in the county of Cavan, who protested to me that he never knew above one or two instances under the age of six, even in a part of the kingdom so renowned for the quickest proficiency in that art.

I am assured by our merchants that a boy or girl before twelve years old is no salable commodity; and even when they come to this age, they will not yield above three pounds, or three pounds and half a crown at most on the exchange; which cannot turn to account either to the parents or the kingdom, the charge of nutriment and rags having been at least four times that value.

I shall now therefore humbly propose my own thoughts, which I hope will not be liable to the least objection.

I have been assured by a very knowing American of my acquaintance in London, that a young healthy child well nursed is at a year old a most delicious, nourishing, and wholesome food, whether stewed, roasted, baked, or boiled; and I make no doubt that it will equally serve in a fricassee or a ragout.

I do therefore humbly offer it to public consideration that of the hundred and twenty thousand children, already computed, twenty thousand may be reserved for breed, whereof only one-fourth part to be males, which is more than we allow to sheep, black cattle, or swine; and my reason is that these children are seldom the fruits of marriage, a circumstance not much regarded by our savages, therefore one male will be sufficient to serve four females. That the remaining hundred thousand may at a year old be offered in sale to the persons of quality and fortune through the kingdom, always advising the mother to let them suck plentifully in the last month, so as to render them plump and fat for a good table. A child will make two dishes at an entertainment for friends; and when the family dines alone, the fore or hind quarter will make a reasonable dish, and seasoned with a little pepper or salt will be very good boiled on the fourth day, especially in winter.

I have reckoned upon a medium that a child just born will weigh twelve pounds, and in a solar year if tolerably nursed increased to twenty-eight pounds.

I grant this food will be somewhat dear, and therefore very proper for landlords, who, as they have already devoured most of the parents, seem to have the best title to the children.

Infant's flesh will be in season throughout the year, but more plentiful in March, and a little before and after. For we are told by a grave author, an eminent French physician, that fish being a prolific diet, there are more children born in Roman Catholic countries about nine months after Lent than at any other season: therefore, reckoning a year after Lent, the markets will be more glutted than usual, because the number of popish infants is at least three to one in this kingdom; and therefore it will have one other collateral advantage, by lessening the number of Papists among us.

I have already computed the charge of nursing a beggar's child (in which list I reckon all cottagers, laborers, and four fifths of the farmers) to be about two shillings per annum, rags included: and I believe no gentleman would repine to give ten shillings for the carcass of a good fat child, which, as I have said, will make four dishes of excellent nutritive meat, when he hath only some particular friend or his own family to dine with him. Thus the squire will learn to be a good landlord, and grow popular among the tenants; the mother will have eight shillings net profit, and be fit for work till she produces another child.

Those who are more thrifty (as I must confess the times require) may flay the carcass; the skin of which artificially dressed will make admirable gloves for ladies, and summer boots for fine gentlemen.

As to our city of Dublin, shambles may be appointed for this purpose in the most convenient parts of it, and butchers we may be assured will not be wanting; although I rather recommend buying the children alive, and dressing them hot from the knife as we do roasting pigs.

A very worthy person, a true lover of his country, and whose virtues I highly esteem, was lately pleased in discoursing on this matter to offer a refinement upon my scheme. He said that many gentlemen of this kingdom, having of late destroyed their deer, he conceived that the want of venison might be well supplied by the bodies of young lads and maidens, not exceeding fourteen years of age nor under twelve, so great a number of both sexes in every county being now ready to starve for want of work and service; and these to be disposed of by their parents, if alive, or otherwise by their nearest relations. But with due deference to so excellent a friend and so deserving a patriot, I cannot be altogether in his sentiments; for as to the males, my American acquaintance assured me from frequent experience that their flesh was generally tough and lean, like that of our schoolboys, by continual exercise, and their taste disagreeable; and to fatten them would not answer the charge. Then as to the females, it would, I think with humble submission, be a loss to the public, because they soon would become breeders themselves: and besides, it is not improbable that some scrupulous people might be apt to censure such a practice (although indeed very unjustly) as a little bordering upon cruelty; which, I confess, hath always been with me the strongest objection against any project, how well so ever intended.

But in order to justify my friend, he confessed that this expedient was put into his head by the famous Psalmanazar, a native of the island Formosa, who came from thence to

London above twenty years ago, and in conversation told my friend that in his country when any young person happened to be put to death, the executioner sold the carcass to persons of quality as a prime dainty; and that in his time the body of a plump girl of fifteen, who was crucified for an attempt to poison the emperor, was sold to his Imperial Majesty's prime minister of state, and other great mandarins of the court, in joints from the gibbet, at four hundred crowns. Neither indeed can I deny that if the same use were made of several plump young girls in this town, who without one single groat to their fortunes cannot stir abroad without a chair, and appear at the playhouse and assemblies in foreign fineries which they never will pay for, the kingdom would not be the worse.

Some persons of a desponding spirit are in great concern about that vast number of poor people who are aged, diseased, or maimed, and I have been desired to employ my thoughts what course may be taken to ease the nation of so grievous an encumbrance. But I am not in the least pain upon that matter, because it is very well known that they are every day dying and rotting by cold and famine, and filth and vermin, as fast as can be reasonably expected. And as to the younger laborers, they are now in almost as hopeful a condition. They cannot get work, and consequently pine away for want of nourishment to a degree that if at any time they are accidentally hired to common labor, they have not strength to perform it; and thus the country and themselves are happily delivered from the evils to come.

I have too long digressed, and therefore shall return to my subject. I think the advantages by the proposal which I have made are obvious and many, as well as of the highest importance.

For first, as I have already observed, it would greatly lessen the number of Papists, with whom we are yearly overrun, being the principal breeders of the nation as well as our most dangerous enemies; and who stay at home on purpose to deliver the kingdom to the Pretender, hoping to take their advantage by the absence of so many good Protestants, who have chosen rather to leave their country than to stay at home and pay tithes against their conscience to an Episcopal curate.

Secondly, the poorer tenants will have something valuable of their own, which by law may be made liable to distress, and help to pay their landlord's rent, their corn and cattle being already seized and money a thing unknown.

Thirdly, whereas the maintenance of an hundred thousand children, from two years old and upward, cannot be computed at less than ten shillings a piece per annum, the nation's stock will be thereby increased fifty thousand pounds per annum, besides the profit of a new dish introduced to the tables of all gentlemen of fortune in the kingdom who have any refinement in taste. And the money will circulate among ourselves, the goods being entirely of our own growth and manufacture.

Fourthly, the constant breeders, besides the gain of eight shillings sterling per annum by the sale of their children, will be rid of the charge of maintaining them after the first year.

Fifthly, this food would likewise bring great custom to taverns, where the vintners will certainly be so prudent as to procure the best receipts for dressing it to perfection, and consequently have their houses frequented by all the fine gentlemen, who justly value themselves upon their knowledge in good eating; and a skillful cook, who understands how to oblige his guests, will contrive to make it as expensive as they please.

Sixthly, this would be a great inducement to marriage, which all wise nations have either encouraged by rewards or enforced by laws and penalties. It would increase the care and tenderness of mothers toward their children, when they were sure of a settlement for life to the poor babes, provided in some sort by the public, to their annual profit instead of expense. We should see an honest emulation among the married women, which of them could bring the fattest child to the market. Men would become as fond of their wives during the time of their pregnancy as they are now of their mares in foal, their cows in calf, or sows when they are ready to farrow; nor offer to beat or kick them (as is too frequent a practice) for fear of a miscarriage.

Many other advantages might be enumerated. For instance, the addition of some thousand carcasses in our exportation of barreled beef, the propagation of swine's flesh, and improvement in the art of making good bacon, so much wanted among us by the great destruction of pigs, too frequent at our tables, which are no way comparable in taste or magnificence to a well-grown, fat yearling child, which roasted whole will make a considerable figure at a lord mayor's feast or any other public entertainment. But this and many others I omit, being studious of brevity.

Supposing that one thousand families in this city would be constant customers for infants' flesh, besides others who might have it at merry meetings, particularly weddings and christenings, compute that Dublin would take off annually about twenty thousand carcasses, and the rest of the kingdom (where probably they will be sold somewhat cheaper) the remaining eighty thousand.

I can think of no one objection that will possibly be raised against this proposal, unless it should be urged that the number of people will be thereby much lessened in the kingdom. This I freely own, and it was indeed one principal design in offering it to this world. I desire the reader will observe, that I calculate my remedy for this one individual kingdom of Ireland and for no other that ever was, is, or I think ever can be upon earth. Therefore let no man talk to me of other expedients: of taxing our absentees at five shillings a pound: of using neither clothes nor household furniture except what is of our own growth and manufacture: of utterly rejecting the materials and instruments that promote foreign luxury: of curing the expensiveness of pride, vanity, idleness, and gaming in our women: of introducing a vein of parsimony, prudence, and temperance: of learning to love our country, in the want of which we differ even from Laplanders and the inhabitants of Topinamboo: of quitting our animosities and factions, nor acting any longer like the Jews, who were murdering one another at the very moment their city was taken: of being a little cautious not to sell our country and conscience for nothing: of teaching landlords to have at least one degree of mercy toward their tenants: lastly, of putting a spirit of honesty, industry, and skill into our shopkeepers; who, if a resolution could be now taken to buy only our native goods, would immediately unite to cheat and exact upon us in the price, the measure, and the goodness, nor could ever yet be brought to make one fair proposal of just dealing, though often and earnestly invited to it.

Therefore I repeat, let no man talk to me of these and the like expedients, till he hath at least some glimpse of hope that there will ever be some hearty and sincere attempt to put them in practice.

But as to myself, having been wearied out for many years with offering vain, idle, visionary thoughts, and at length utterly despairing of success, I fortunately fell upon this proposal, which, as it is wholly new, so it hath something solid and real, of no expense and little trouble, full in our own power, and whereby we can incur no danger in disobliging England. For this kind of commodity will not bear exportation, the flesh being of too tender a consistence to admit a long continuance in salt, although perhaps I could name a country which would be glad to eat up our whole nation without it.

After all, I am not so violently bent upon my own opinion as to reject any offer proposed by wise men, which shall be found equally innocent, cheap, easy, and effectual. But before something of that kind shall be advanced in contradiction to my scheme, and offering a better, I desire the author or authors will be pleased maturely to consider two points. First, as things now stand, how they will be able to find food and raiment for an hundred thousand useless mouths and backs. And secondly, there being a round million of creatures in human figure throughout this kingdom, whose sole subsistence put into a common stock would leave them in debt two millions of pounds sterling, adding those who are beggars by profession to the bulk of farmers, cottagers, and laborers, with their wives and children who are beggars in effect; I desire those politicians who dislike my overture, and may perhaps be so bold to attempt an answer, that they will first ask the parents of these mortals whether they would not at this day think it a great happiness to have been sold for food at a year old in the manner I prescribe, and thereby have avoided such a perpetual scene of misfortunes as they have since gone through by the oppression of landlords, the impossibility of paying rent without money or trade, the want of common sustenance, with neither house nor clothes to cover them from the inclemencies of the weather, and the most inevitable prospect of entailing the like or greater miseries upon their breed forever.

I profess, in the sincerity of my heart, that I have not the least personal interest in endeavoring to promote this necessary work, having no other motive than the public good of my country, by advancing our trade, providing for infants, relieving the poor, and giving some pleasure to the rich. I have no children by which I can propose to get a single penny; the youngest being nine years old, and my wife past childbearing.

Mother Tongue

Amy Tan

I am not a scholar of English or literature. I cannot give you much more than personal opinions on the English language and its variations in this country or others. I am a writer. And by that definition, I am someone who has always loved language. I am fascinated by language in daily life. I spend a great deal of my time thinking about the power of language—the way it can evoke an emotion, a visual image, a complex idea, or a simple truth. Language is the tool of my trade. And I use them all—all the Englishes I grew up with. Recently, I was made keenly aware of the different Englishes I do use. I was giving a talk to a large group of people, the same talk I had already given to half a dozen other groups. The talk was about my writing, my life, and my book *The Joy Luck Club,* and it was going along well enough, until I remembered one major difference that made the whole talk sound wrong. My mother was in the room. And it was perhaps the first time she had heard me give a lengthy speech, using the kind of English I have never used with her. I was saying things like "the intersection of memory and imagination" and "There is an aspect of my Fiction that relates to thus-and-thus"—a speech filled with carefully wrought grammatical phrases, burdened, it suddenly seemed to me, with nominalized forms, past perfect tenses, conditional phrases, forms of standard English that I had learned in school and through books, the forms of English I did not use at home with my mother. Just last week, as I was walking down the street with her, I again found myself conscious of the English I was using, the English I do use with her. We were talking about the price of new and used furniture, and I heard myself saying this: "Not waste money that way." My husband was with us as well, and he didn't notice any switch in my English. And then I realized why. It's because over the twenty years, we've been together I've often used the same kind of English with him, and sometimes he even uses it with me. It has become our language of intimacy, a different sort of English that relates to family talk, the language I grew up with.

Language Barriers

You should know that my mother's expressive command of English belies how much she actually understands. She reads the Forbes report, listens to Wall Street Week, converses daily with her stockbroker, reads Shirley MacLaine's books with ease—all kinds of things I can't begin to understand. Yet some of my friends tell me they understand 50% of what my mother says. Some say they understand 80%–90%. Some say they understand none of it, as if she were speaking pure Chinese. But to me, my mother's English is perfectly clear, perfectly natural. It's my mother tongue. Her language, as I hear it, is vivid, direct, full of observation and imagery. That was the language that helped shape the way I saw things, expressed things, made sense of the world. Lately I've been giving more thought to the kind of English my mother speaks. Like others, I have described it to people as "broken" or "fractured" English. But I wince when I say that. It has always bothered me that I can think of no way to describe it other than "broken," as if it were damaged and needed to be fixed, as if it lacked a certain wholeness and soundness. I've heard other terms used, "limited English," for example. But they seem just as bad, as if everything is limited, including people's perceptions of the limited English speaker. I know this for a fact, because when I was growing up, my mother's "limited" English limited my perception of her. I was ashamed of her English. I believed that her English reflected the quality of what she had to say. That is, because she expressed them imperfectly, her thoughts were imperfect. And I had plenty of empirical evidence to support me: the fact that people in department stores, at banks, and in restaurants did not take her seriously, did not give her good service, pretended not to understand her, or even acted as if they did not hear her. My mother has long realized the limitations of her English as well. When I was a teenager, she used to have me call people on the phone and pretend I was she. In this guise, I was forced to ask for information or even to complain and yell at people who had been rude to her. One time it was a call to her stockbroker in New York. She had cashed out her small portfolio, and it just so happened we were going to New York the next week, our first trip outside California. I had to get on the phone and say in an adolescent voice that was not very convincing, "This is Mrs. Tan." My mother was standing in the back whispering loudly, "Why he don't send me check, already two weeks late. So mad he lie to me, losing me money." And then I said in perfect English on the phone, "Yes, I'm getting rather concerned. You had agreed to send the check two weeks ago, but it hasn't arrived." Then she began to talk more loudly. "What he want, I come to New York tell him font of his boss, you cheating me?" And I was trying to calm her down, make her be quiet, while telling the stockbroker. "I can't tolerate any more excuses. If I don't receive the check immediately, I am going to have to speak to your manager when I'm in New York next week." And sure enough, the following week, there we were in front of this astonished stockbroker, and I was sitting there red-faced and quiet, and my mother, the real Mrs. Tan, was shouting at his boss in her impeccable broken English.

Blending Old and New

Lately I've been asked, as a writer, why there are not more Asian-Americans represented in American literature. Why are there few Asian-Americans enrolled in creative writing programs? Why do so many Chinese students go into engineering? Well, these are broad sociological questions I can't begin to answer. But I have noticed in surveys—in fact, just last week—that Asian-American students, as a whole, do significantly better on math achievement tests than on English tests. And this makes me think that there are other Asian-American students whose English spoken in the home might also be described as "broken" or "limited." And perhaps I began to write stories using all the Englishes I grew up with. they also have teachers who are steering them away from writing and into math and science, which is what happened to me. Fortunately, I happen to be rebellious and enjoy the challenge of disproving assumptions made about me. I became an English major my first year in college, after being enrolled as premed. I started writing nonfiction as a freelancer the week after I was told by my boss at the time that writing was my worst skill and I should hone my talents toward account management. But it wasn't until 1985 that I began to write fiction. At first, I wrote what I thought to be wittily crafted sentences, sentences that would finally prove I had mastery over the English language. Here's an example from the first draft of a story that later made its way into *The Joy Luck Club*, but without this line: "That was my mental quandary in its nascent state." A terrible line, which I can barely pronounce.

Fortunately, for reasons I won't get into here, I later decided I should envision a reader for the stories I would write. And the reader I decided on was my mother, because these were stories about mothers. So with this reader in mind—and in fact she did read my early drafts—I began to write stories using all the Englishes I grew up with: the English I spoke to my mother, which for lack of a better term might be described as "simple"; the English she used with me, which for lack of a better term might be described as "broken"; my translation of her Chinese, which could certainly be described as "watered down"; and what I imagined to be her translation of her Chinese if she could speak in perfect English, her internal language, and for that I sought to preserve the essence, but neither an English nor a Chinese structure. I wanted to capture what language ability tests could never reveal: her intent, her passion, her imagery, the rhythms of her speech, and the nature of her thoughts. Apart from what any critic had to say about my writing. I knew I had succeeded where it counted when my mother finished reading my book and gave me her verdict: "So easy to read."

Walden (excerpted)

Henry David Thoreau

Morning is when I am awake and there is a dawn in me. Moral reform is the effort to throw off sleep. Why is it that men give so poor an account of their day if they have not been slumbering? They are not such poor calculators. If they had not been overcome with drowsiness, they would have performed something. The millions are awake enough for physical labor; but only one in a million is awake enough for effective in intellectual exertion, only one in a hundred millions to a poetic or divine life. To be awake is to be alive. I have never yet met a man who was quite awake. How could I have looked him in the face?

We must learn to reawaken and keep ourselves awake, not by mechanical aids, but by an infinite expectation of the dawn, which does not forsake us in our soundest sleep. I know of no more encouraging fact than the unquestionable ability of man to elevate his life by a conscious endeavor. It is something to be able to paint a particular picture, or to carve a statue, and so to make a few objects beautiful; but it is far more glorious to carve and paint the very atmosphere and medium through which we look, which morally we can do. To affect the quality of the day, that is the highest of arts. Every man is tasked to make his life, even in its details, worthy of the contemplation of his most elevated and critical hour. If we refused, or rather used up, such paltry information as we get, the oracles would distinctly inform us how this might be done.

I went to the woods because I wished to live deliberately, to front only the essential facts of life, and see if I could not learn what it had to teach, and not, when I came to die, discover that I had not lived. I did not wish to live what was not life, living is so dear; nor did I wish to practice resignation, unless it was quite necessary. I wanted to live deep and suck out all the marrow of life, to live so sturdily and Spartan-like as to put to rout all that was not life, to cut a broad swath and shave close, to drive life into a corner, and reduce it to its lowest terms, and, if it proved to be mean, why then to get the whole and genuine meanness of it, and publish its meanness to the world; or if it were sublime, to know it by experience, and be able to give a true account of it in my next excursion. For most men, it appears to me, are in a strange uncertainty about it, whether it is of the devil or of God, and have *somewhat hastily* concluded that it is the chief end of man here to "glorify God and enjoy him forever."

* * *

I left the woods for as good a reason as I went there. Perhaps it seemed to me that I had several more lives to live, and could not spare any more time for that one. It is remarkable how easily and insensibly we fall into a particular route, and make a beaten track for ourselves. I had not lived there a week before my feet wore a path from my door to the pondside; and though it is five or six years since I trod it, it is still quite distinct. It is true, I fear that others may have fallen into it, and so helped to keep it open. The surface of the

Source: From *Walden and Civil Disobedience* by Henry David Thoreau, 1849.

earth is soft and impressible by the feet of men; and so with the paths which the mind travels. How worn and dusty, then, must be the highways of the world, how deep the ruts of tradition and conformity! I did not wish to take a cabin passage, but rather to go before the mast and on the deck of the world, for there I could best see the moonlight amid the mountains. I do not wish to go below now.

I learned this, at least, by my experiment; that if one advances confidently in the direction of his dreams, and endeavors to live the life he has imagined, he will meet with a success unexpected in common hours. He will put some things behind, will pass an invisible boundary; new, universal, and more liberal laws will begin to establish themselves around and within him; or the old laws be expanded, and interpreted in his favor in a more liberal sense, and he will live with the license of a higher order of beings. In proportion as he simplifies his life, the laws of the universe will appear less complex, and solitude will not be solitude, nor poverty, nor weakness. If you have built castles in the air, your work need not be lost; that is where they should be. Now put the foundations under them.

* * *

However mean your life is, meet it and live it; do not shun it and call it hard names. It is not so bad as you are. It looks poorest when you are richest. The faultfinder will find faults even in paradise. Love your life, poor as it is. You may perhaps have some pleasant, thrilling, glorious hours, even in a poorhouse. The setting sun is reflected from the windows of the almshouse as brightly as from the rich man's abode; the snow melts before its door as early in the spring. I do not see but a quiet mind may live as contentedly there, and have as cheering thoughts, as in a palace. The town's poor seem to me often to live the most independent lives of any. May be they are simply great enough to receive without misgiving. Most think that they are above being supported by the town; but it oftener happens that they are not above supporting themselves by dishonest means, which should be more disreputable. Cultivate poverty like a garden herb, like sage. Do not trouble yourself much to get new things, whether clothes or friends. Turn the old; return to them. Things do not change; we change. Sell your clothes and keep your thoughts. God will see that you do not want society. If I were confined to a corner of a garret all my days, like a spider, the world would be just as large to me while I had my thoughts about me. The philosopher said: "From an army of three divisions one can take away its general, and put it in disorder; from the man the most abject and vulgar one cannot take away his thought." Do not seek so anxiously to be developed, to subject yourself to many influences to be played on; it is all dissipation. Humility like darkness reveals the heavenly lights. The shadows of poverty and meanness gather around us, "and lo! creation widens to our view." We are often reminded that if there were bestowed on us the wealth of Croesus, our aims must still be the same, and our means essentially the same. Moreover, if you are restricted in your range by poverty, if you cannot buy books and newspapers, for instance, you are but confined to the most significant and vital experiences; you are compelled to deal with the material which yields the most sugar and the most starch. It is life near the bone where it is sweetest. You are defended from being a trifler. No man loses ever on a lower level by magnanimity on a higher. Superfluous wealth can buy superfluities only. Money is not required to buy one necessary of the soul.

Simplicity

William Zinsser

Clutter is the disease of American writing. We are a society strangling in unnecessary words, circular constructions, pompous frills, and meaningless jargon.

Who can understand the viscous language of everyday American commerce and enterprise: the business letter, the interoffice memo, the corporation report, the notice from the the bank explaining its latest "simplified" statement? What member of an insurance or medical plan can decipher the brochure that tells him what his costs and benefits are? What father or mother can put together a child's toy—on Christmas Eve or any other eve—from the instructions on the box? Our national tendency is to inflate and thereby sound important. The airline pilot who wakes us to announce that he is presently anticipating experiencing considerable weather wouldn't dream of saying that there's a storm ahead and it may get bumpy. The sentence is too simple—there must be something wrong with it.

But the secret of good writing is to strip every sentence to its cleanest components. Every word that serves no function, every long word that could be a short word, every adverb which carries the same meaning that is already in the verb, every passive construction that leaves the reader unsure of who is doing what—these are the thousand and one adulterants that weaken the strength of a sentence. And they usually occur, ironically, in proportion to education and rank.

During the late 1960s, the president of a major university wrote a letter to mollify the alumni after a spell of campus unrest. "You are probably aware," he began, "that we have been experiencing very considerable potentially explosive expressions of dissatisfaction on issues only partially related." He meant that the students had been hassling them about different things. I was far more upset by the president's English than by the students' potentially explosive expressions of dissatisfaction. I would have preferred the presidential approach oaken by Franklin D. Roosevelt when he tried to convert into English his own government's memos, such as this blackout order of 1942:

Such preparations shall be made as will completely obscure all Federal buildings and non-Federal buildings occupied by the Federal government during an air raid for any period of time from visibility by reason of internal or external illumination.

"Tell them," Roosevelt said, "that in buildings where they have to keep the work going to put something across the windows."

Simplify, simplify. Thoreau said it, as we are so often reminded, and no American writer more consistently practiced what he preached. Open Walden to any page and you will find a man saying in a plain and orderly way what is on his mind:

I love to be alone. I never found the companion that was so companionable as solitude. We are for the most part more lonely when we go abroad among men than when we stay in our chambers. A man thinking or working always alone, let him be where he will. Solitude is not measured by the miles that intervene between a man and his fellows. The really diligent student in the crowded hives of Cambridge College is as solitary as a dervish in the desert.

How can the rest of us achieve such enviable freedom from clutter? The answer is to clear our heads of clutter. Clear thinking becomes clear writing: one can't exist without the other. It is impossible for a muddy thinker to write good English. He may get away with it for a paragraph or two, but soon the reader will be lost, and there is no sin so grave, for he will not easily be lured back.

Who is this elusive creature the reader? He is a person with an attention span of about twenty seconds. He is assailed on every side by forces competing for his time: by newspapers and magazines, by television and radio and stereo, by his wife and children and pets, by his house and his yard and all the gadgets that he has bought to keep them spruce, and by that most potent of competitors, sleep. The man snoozing in his chair with an unfinished magazine open on his lap is a man who was being given too much unnecessary trouble by the writer.

It won't do to say that the snoozing reader is too dumb or too lazy to keep pace with the train of thought. My sympathies are with him. If the reader is lost, it is generally because the writer has not been careful enough to keep him on the path.

This carelessness can take any number of forms. Perhaps a sentence is so excessively cluttered that the reader, hacking his way through the verbiage, simply doesn't know what it means. Perhaps a sentence has been so shoddily constructed that the reader could read it in any of several ways. Perhaps the writer has switched pronouns in mid-sentence, or has switched tenses, so the reader loses track of who is talking or when the action took place. Perhaps Sentence B is not a logical sequel to Sentence A—the writer, in whose head the connection is clear, has not bothered to provide the missing link. Perhaps the writer has used an important word incorrectly by not taking the trouble to look it up. He may think that "sanguine" and "sanguinary" mean the same thing, but the difference is a bloody big one. The reader can only infer (speaking of big differences) what the writer is trying to imply.

Faced with these obstacles, the reader is at first a remarkably tenacious bird. He blames himself—he obviously missed something, and he goes back over the mystifying sentence, or over the whole paragraph, piecing it out like an ancient rule, making guesses, and moving on. But he won't do this for long. The writer is making him work too hard, and the reader will look for one who is better at his craft.

The writer must therefore constantly ask himself: What am I trying to say? Surprisingly often, he doesn't know. Then he must look at what he has written and ask: Have I said it? Is it clear to someone encountering the subject for the first time? If it's not, it is because some fuzz has worked its way into the machinery. The clear writer is a person clearheaded enough to see this stuff for what it is: fuzz.

I don't mean that some people are born clearheaded and are therefore natural writers, whereas others are naturally fuzzy and will never write well. Thinking clearly is a conscious act that the writer must force upon himself, just as if he were embarking on any other project that requires logic: adding up a laundry list or doing an algebra problem. Good writing doesn't come naturally, though most people obviously think it does. The professional writer is forever being bearded by strangers who say that they'd like to "try a little writing sometime" when they retire from their real profession. Good writing takes self-discipline and, very often, self-knowledge.

Many writers, for instance, can't stand to throw anything away. Their sentences are littered with words that mean essentially the same thing and with phrases which make a point that is implicit in what they have already said. When students give me these littered sentences, I beg them to select from the surfeit of words the few that most precisely fit what they want to say. Choose one, I plead, from among the three almost identical adjectives. Get rid of the unnecessary adverbs. Eliminate "in a funny sort of way" and other such qualifiers they do no useful work.

The students look stricken—I am taking all their wonderful words away. I am only taking their superfluous words away, leaving what is organic and strong.

"But," one of my worst offenders confessed, "I never can get rid of anything—you should see my room." (I didn't take him up on the offer.) "I have two lamps where I only need one, but I can't decide which one I like better, so l keep them both." He went on to enumerate his duplicated or unnecessary objects, and over the weeks ahead, I went on throwing away his duplicated and unnecessary words. By the end of the term—a term that he found acutely painful—his sentences were clean.

"I've had to change my whole approach to writing," he told me. "Now I have to think before I start every sentence and I have to think about every word." The very idea amazed him. Whether his room also looked better I never found out.

Writing is hard work. A clear sentence is no accident. Very few sentences come out right the first time. Or the third. Keep thinking and rewriting until you say what you want to say.

APPENDIX OF MARKING TERMS

adj./adv.	adjective (e.g., real) versus adverb (e.g., really)
apos.	apostrophe (misuse of apostrophe or missing apostrophe)
art.	definite article ("the") = specific, or only one, versus indefinite article ("a" or "an") = one
[c]/[u]	mix-up of countable noun (e.g., desk) with uncountable noun (e.g., information)
cap.	capital letter (capitalize proper nouns and most acronyms)
case	pronoun case (subjective, objective, possessive)
cit.	citation format
colloq.	colloquialism (avoid informality)
contr.	contraction (avoid contractions in formal writing)
cs	comma splice (a semicolon, not a comma, should separate independent clauses)
dm or mm	dangling or misplaced modifier (modifiers must go clearly with what they describe)
form.	format
frag.	sentence fragment (not an independent clause)
fs	fused sentence (missing punctuation between independent clauses)
id.	idiom (standard expression)
log.	logic
nsw	no such word

P	paragraphing (e.g., begin new paragraph)
p of s	part of speech (e.g., mistaking a noun for a verb)
pass.	passive voice (use active voice as default in many—though not all—situations)
poss.	possessive form (apostrophe needed for possessive nouns)
prep.	preposition error (e.g., idiom)
pron.	pronoun error (e.g., wrong pronoun, vague pronoun)
punc.	punctuation error (missing or inappropriate punctuation)
//	parallelism (listed items must be grammatically parallel)
Q	question (use a question mark after rhetorical questions)
red.	redundant (eliminate unnecessary words)
r-o	run-on sentence (lacking adequate punctuation, such as necessary commas and semicolons)
s-v	subject-verb agreement
self-ref.	self-referential wording (to you as the writer or to the document itself)
sent. var.	sentence variety (use a variety of grammatical and stylistic types)
sp.	spelling
ss	sentence structure (restructure for clarity)
t	verb tense (consider appropriateness and consistency of tense)
trans./intrans.	transitive versus intransitive verb form (transitive takes a direct object)
transit.	transition (missing or inappropriate)
typo	typographical mistake (careless or unintentional error)
vf	verb form (no such verb tense exists, e.g., did went)
weak expl.	weak expletive sentence structure (e.g., there is . . .)
ww	wrong word (diction error)

CPSIA information can be obtained
at www.ICGtesting.com
Printed in the USA
LVHW062104230619
622086LV00001B/1/P